You Can Work Wonders

A Handbook on Living your Full Potential

Manoj Dembla

Printed in India

IndiePress

ISBN: 978-93-6045-563-7

First Printing, 2024

Indie Press

A division of Nasadiya Technologies Private Ltd.

Koramangala, Bengaluru

Karnataka-560029

http://indiepress.in/

Edited by Anagha Somanakoppa

Typeset by MAP Systems, Bengaluru

Book Cover designed by Sankhasubhro Nath

Publishing Consultant: Deeksha

Acknowledgments

Writing this book has been a journey that would not have been possible without the help and support of many people. I would like to express my deepest gratitude to those who have helped me along the way.

Firstly, I would like to thank my family, Kavita, Komal, Kush, and Richie, for their unwavering support and encouragement. Their love and encouragement have been a constant source of inspiration and I am grateful for their continued support throughout the writing process.

I would also like to thank my editor and publisher for their guidance, expertise, and support. Their insight and feedback have been invaluable in helping me refine my ideas and bring this book to life.

I would also like to extend my gratitude to many experts and professionals who shared their knowledge and expertise with me. Their insights and perspectives have been instrumental in shaping the content of this book and helping me share You Can Work Wonders with the world.

Finally, I would like to thank my readers. It is my hope that this book will inspire and motivate you to tap your energies to unleash your full potential. Your support and feedback are greatly appreciated and I look forward to hearing your thoughts on this book.

Thank you all for your support and encouragement. You can work wonders. This is just the beginning and I am excited to continue exploring this exciting and transformative journey together.

Preface

Have you ever felt like you're not living up to your full potential? Do you ever find yourself wondering what you could achieve if you just had the right tools and strategies? If so, this book is for you.

'You Can Work Wonders: A Handbook on Living Your Full Potential' is a practical guide to achieving personal and professional success. Whether you're just starting out in your career or looking to take your skills and accomplishments to the next level, this book will provide you with the tools, strategies, and inspiration you need to achieve your goals.

Throughout the book, you'll find practical advice on topics such as goal-setting, time management, productivity, self-care, mindfulness, and more. Each chapter is designed to help you identify your strengths and weaknesses, develop a plan for achieving your goals, and take action towards achieving your full potential.

In addition to practical advice, this book also includes personal stories and insights from individuals who have achieved success in their own lives. These stories serve as inspiration and motivation, demonstrating that with hard work, determination, and the right mindset, anyone can achieve their goals and live a fulfilling and meaningful life.

Ultimately, this book is about empowering you to take control of your life and achieve your full potential. It's about recognizing your strengths, overcoming your limitations, and living a life that is both fulfilling and meaningful. We hope that the insights, strategies, and inspiration provided in this book will help you on your journey towards achieving your full potential and living your best life.

Contents

Chapter 1

The Wonders Within

Unveiling Your Inner Potential

In the vast expanse of your being lies a reservoir of untapped potential, a wellspring of greatness waiting to surge forth. Today, we embark on a transformative journey— a journey to unveil the sheer magnitude of your inner capabilities.

It's time to shed the cloak of self-doubt and stand naked before the mirror of self-discovery. Peel away the layers that conceal your brilliance, for within you resides a force that can move mountains. Embrace the revelation that you are a powerhouse of untold potential.

Embark on this expedition with the spirit of an adventurer. Navigate the uncharted territories of your passions, dreams, and aspirations. Uncover the hidden talents that lie dormant, waiting for the call to action. Be bold, be fearless— for it is in the fearless pursuit of our potential that we discover our true selves.

Picture yourself as a constellation of strengths, each star shining brightly in the cosmos of your existence. Identify and embrace these strengths, for they are the celestial forces that will guide you on your journey. Illuminating your strengths will not only light your path but also inspire those around you.

In the pursuit of your potential, challenges will inevitably arise. They are not roadblocks but stepping stones, opportunities to showcase the resilience that resides within you. Embrace challenges as catalysts for growth, for it is through adversity that diamonds are forged.

Unveiling your potential is not a passive act; it requires purposeful action. Take deliberate steps toward your goals. Every action, no matter how small, is a testament to your commitment to self-realization. As you take charge of your journey, witness the transformation unfold.

Confidence is the beacon that signals the world to acknowledge your presence. Stand tall in the knowing that you are a force to be reckoned with. Let your confidence radiate, illuminating not only your path but inspiring others to embark on their journeys of self-discovery.

As you uncover the layers and reveal the radiant core of your potential, take a moment to celebrate. You are a masterpiece in the making, a canvas painted with the hues of your unique abilities. Revel in the joy of self-discovery, for you are on the brink of greatness.

Unveiling your inner potential is not a one-time event but a continual process. As you peel back the layers, remember that the journey is as significant as the destination. Embrace the unveiling with an open heart, a courageous spirit, and an unshakeable belief that within you, wonders are waiting to be unleashed. Today marks the beginning of your transformation—embrace it, live it, and watch as your inner brilliance illuminates the world.

Exploring the Depths of Self-Discovery

In the expansive tapestry of life, an uncharted journey beckons—one that delves deep into the recesses of your own existence. "Navigating the Depths: A Journey into Self-Discovery" isn't a mere expedition; it's a transformative odyssey, a quest into the very core of your being.

Picture your soul as an unexplored ocean, filled with treasures waiting to be unveiled. This inner odyssey is your opportunity to strip away layers of societal expectations, self-doubt, and external influences. It's about rediscovering the authentic essence that defines you.

Amidst the hustle and bustle of life, pause to reflect. Your thoughts, dreams, and desires are not random ripples; they are your compass, guiding you to undiscovered territories within. Embrace introspection as you navigate the vastness of your inner world.

As you delve deeper, you may encounter shadows—doubts, fears, and insecurities. Fear not, for it is in confronting these shadows that you gain the strength to navigate even the darkest depths. Embrace the process of facing your fears, for therein lies the key to unlocking your true potential.

Within the depths, you'll find the currents of passion—your driving force. Identify what ignites the flame within you. Whether it's a long-lost hobby, an unfulfilled dream, or a creative pursuit, allow your passions to be the wind in your sails, propelling you forward on this profound journey.

Resilience becomes your anchor amidst the sometimes turbulent waters. Embrace setbacks as lessons, for they are the waves that sculpt the strength of your character.

On this journey, perfection is not the destination. It's about progress—every step forward is a triumph. Celebrate the small victories, relish the lessons learned, and understand that the beauty of self-discovery lies in the ongoing process, not a flawless outcome.

The depths of self-discovery are boundless, and as you sail through uncharted waters, embrace the unknown with open arms. Life's mysteries are not obstacles but invitations to explore the unexplored realms of your own potential.

In the silence of self-discovery, find your voice. Express your thoughts, dreams, and aspirations. Your story is uniquely yours, and by sharing it, you not only empower yourself but also inspire others to embark on their own journeys of self-discovery.

This book is an invitation to embark on a transformative expedition—one that promises not just self-awareness but a profound connection with the extraordinary individual that you are. As you sail through the currents of introspection, resilience, and passion, may you uncover the treasures that make you, unequivocally, you. The journey is yours, and the discoveries are boundless—set sail and explore the depths within.

Recognizing the Hidden Strengths That Await Activation

In the intricate mosaic of your existence, there lies a reservoir of latent power awaiting activation—hidden strengths pulsating beneath the surface, yearning to be recognized. Today, we embark on a profound exploration into the depths of your being, not as a mere observer but as an active participant in the unveiling of your dormant capabilities.

Recognizing these hidden strengths is akin to discovering a cache of treasures long forgotten. It requires a deliberate shift in perspective, an intentional gaze into the mirror of self-awareness. Understand that your journey is not a quest for external validation but a revelation of the untapped potential that resides within you.

As you navigate the corridors of your past, present, and future, pay attention to moments where you exhibited resilience, courage, and unwavering determination. These are the footprints of your hidden strengths, signaling their existence in your life.

Embrace the challenges you've overcome, for they are not just hurdles but stepping stones that reveal the tenacity woven into the fabric of your character. Your ability to endure, adapt, and persevere in the face of adversity is a testament to the reservoir of strength that lies within.

Recognizing hidden strengths goes beyond acknowledging past victories; it requires a present moment awareness of your unique qualities. Take stock of your talents, skills, and passions. What activities make your heart race with excitement? What skills do you effortlessly wield? These are the clues pointing to the dormant strengths awaiting activation.

Consider the feedback and affirmations you've received from others. Often, those around you recognize your strengths before you fully do. Listen to the compliments, the expressions of admiration, and the acknowledgments.

They are mirrors reflecting the brilliance of your hidden strengths.

Activation begins with belief—in yourself and in the potential that lies within. Cultivate a mindset that acknowledges your strengths as assets, not accidents. Understand that your unique blend of abilities is a gift to be embraced and unleashed upon the world.

The journey of recognizing and activating hidden strengths is not a sprint but a marathon. It requires patience, self-compassion, and a commitment to continuous growth. As you traverse this path, celebrate the small victories, the milestones, and the moments of self-discovery.

In recognizing the hidden strengths that await activation, you step into a realm of personal empowerment. You become the architect of your destiny, wielding the tools of your strengths to carve out a life rich in purpose and fulfillment. Embrace the journey, for within it lies the extraordinary potential that is uniquely and unequivocally yours.

Anecdote Episode - 1

In the bustling city of Ahmedabad, Gujarat, Ela Bhatt's story unfolded against a backdrop of unspoken struggles faced by women in the unorganized sector. Born in 1933, Ela's early life was marked by a profound sense of justice and a desire to understand the intricate threads that wove through the lives of countless women, hidden in the shadows of society.

After completing her law degree, Ela stood at a crossroads where a conventional path awaited her. However, the unseen threads of injustice, inequality, and unmet potential beckoned to her. Driven by an innate sense of purpose, Ela chose a different journey—one that would redefine the very fabric of women's lives in India.

In the late 1960s, with unwavering determination and a vision for change, Ela embarked on a mission that would become a revolution—the creation of the Self-Employed Women's Association, or SEWA. This marked the beginning of a transformative journey, recognizing that economic empowerment held the key to unlocking the hidden potential within marginalized communities.

The early days of SEWA were a tapestry of challenges, akin to a weaver facing an intricate pattern with uncertainties at every turn. Ela faced skepticism from those who doubted the feasibility of empowering women in the unorganized sector. Financial constraints added threads of uncertainty, and societal norms questioned the unconventional path she had chosen.

Yet, like a skilled weaver navigating through the complexities of her craft, Ela persevered. She became the architect of an organization that would not only challenge societal norms but also redefine the possibilities for countless women. Ela's leadership was a testament to her ability to navigate the delicate intricacies of social change, acknowledging the uniqueness of each woman's story.

Through SEWA, Ela Bhatt provided a platform for women to not only recognize their hidden strengths but also to weave a new narrative for themselves. The organization became a loom of empowerment, where women from the unorganized sector, often relegated to the shadows, could step into the light and showcase their skills, resilience, and potential.

Ela's journey was not just a personal quest but a revolutionary act of weaving together the aspirations, dreams, and strengths of an entire community. Her story teaches us that true empowerment is a gradual process, much like the patient creation of a beautiful painting, stroke by stroke.

In the early threads of SEWA's existence, Ela Bhatt laid the foundation for a movement that continues to unfold, revealing the intricate patterns of empowerment, dignity, and self-reliance. Ela's journey, like the careful crafting of a masterpiece, is a testament to the wonders within, waiting to be discovered and celebrated by those who dare to challenge the status quo and lays the bricks of foundation of empowerment for all.

SEWA became a catalyst for change, empowering women to take charge of their destinies. Ela worked tirelessly to provide them with a platform, a voice, and the means to become self-reliant. The organization embraced the spirit of cooperation, encouraging women to pool their talents and resources.

Ela's leadership was not just about policies and programs; it was about touching lives. She understood that empowerment is not a one-size-fits-all concept. Ela listened to the stories of the women she served, recognizing the unique strengths hidden within each individual.

The impact of SEWA rippled through villages, transforming lives one thread at a time. Women who were once confined to the margins of society emerged as skilled artisans, entrepreneurs, and leaders. Ela's vision of empowerment was not just economic; it was holistic, recognizing the interconnectedness of social, economic, and cultural factors.

As SEWA flourished, Ela's influence extended beyond India's borders. Her philosophy of empowerment inspired movements globally, demonstrating the universality of the human spirit yearning for dignity and self-determination.

Ela Bhatt's story is a testament to the wonders within every individual waiting to be unveiled. She taught us that true empowerment lies in recognizing and activating the hidden strengths that reside within, creating a ripple effect of positive change that transcends generations.

Chapter 2

The Science of Wonder

Understanding the Psychology Behind Achieving Wonders

Unlocking the door to extraordinary achievement involves more than sheer determination; it requires a profound understanding of the psychology that propels us towards wonders. Today, let's embark on a transformative exploration into the intricate workings of the mind and heart, unraveling the mysteries that underpin the journey to greatness.

At its core, the psychology of achieving wonders is a delicate dance between thought and action, belief and manifestation. It commences with cultivating a mindset attuned to the limitless possibilities that life holds. As you gaze into the vast landscape of your goals, perceive them not as distant mountains but as foothills waiting to be conquered.

Belief becomes the cornerstone of this psychological expedition. To achieve wonders, you must first believe in the feasibility of the extraordinary. Your thoughts act as architects, shaping the reality you inhabit. Construct a mental blueprint infused with confidence, positivity, and an unyielding faith in your capabilities.

Visualization emerges as a powerful ally in this psychological arsenal. Envision success with vivid clarity. Feel the emotions, hear the sounds, and immerse yourself in the sensory experience of achieving your goals. This mental rehearsal not only fortifies your belief but also sends ripples into the universe, aligning circumstances to manifest your envisioned wonders.

Yet, understanding the psychology of achievement is not confined to positive thinking alone. It necessitates a nuanced relationship with failure. Rather than viewing setbacks as roadblocks, embrace them as stepping stones. Each stumble is a lesson, and each challenge is an opportunity to refine your approach. Resilience, born from the ashes of failure, propels you further towards your envisioned wonders.

The psychology of achievement also weaves a narrative of intrinsic motivation. Tap into the deep well of passion that resides within you. Passion is the fuel that propels you forward when the road gets arduous. Align your goals with your values, and let the authenticity of your aspirations be the driving force that sustains your journey.

Surrounding yourself with a supportive environment is another crucial aspect of this psychological expedition. Cultivate a network of individuals who uplift, inspire, and challenge you. Human connection is a potent catalyst, infusing your journey with shared energy and collective resilience.

Acknowledging the psychology of achievement means recognizing that wonders are not solitary endeavors; they are collaborative symphonies composed with the harmonies of self-belief, visualization, resilience, passion, and community.

As you navigate this intricate psychology, celebrate the small victories, relish the journey, and revel in the understanding that achieving wonders is not a distant mirage but a dynamic reality sculpted by the profound interplay of your thoughts, actions, and unwavering belief in the extraordinary potential that resides within you. Embrace the psychology of wonders and watch as the ordinary transforms into the extraordinary before your very eyes.

Tapping into the Power of Neuroplasticity

Embarking on the exploration of the human mind reveals a breathtaking landscape shaped by the remarkable phenomenon of neuroplasticity. Within this dynamic symphony of neurons lies the potential for profound personal growth and transformation.

Picture your brain as an ever-changing canvas, continuously adapting and rewiring itself in response to experiences, challenges, and intentional efforts. This malleability, known as neuroplasticity, is the catalyst for unlocking untapped potential and rewriting the narrative of our lives.

To tap into the power of neuroplasticity, engage in deliberate practices that stimulate positive neural pathways. Embrace activities that challenge your mind, learn new skills, and step outside your comfort zone. With each intentional effort, you forge new connections, fortifying pathways that lead to growth and mastery.

Neuroplasticity empowers us to break free from limiting beliefs. Identify and replace self-defeating narratives with empowering thoughts. Repeat positive affirmations, visualize success, and witness how these conscious efforts reshape neural pathways, reinforcing confidence and resilience.

Cultivate a growth mindset, viewing challenges as opportunities for learning and development. In doing so, you activate neuroplasticity to fuel your journey toward continuous improvement. The mind becomes a conscious sculptor, reshaping neural pathways in harmony with a mindset of growth and adaptability.

Mindfulness emerges as a potent tool in the realm of neuroplasticity. By cultivating present-moment awareness, you stimulate regions of the brain associated with emotional regulation, stress reduction, and cognitive flexibility. As the mind becomes a conscious sculptor, the neural pathways reshape in harmony with tranquility and focus.

Human connection serves as a powerful catalyst for neuroplasticity. Engage in meaningful relationships, surround yourself with positive influences, and participate in collaborative endeavors. The exchange of ideas and shared experiences nourishes the brain, fostering an environment ripe for cognitive evolution.

Lifelong learning is the heartbeat of neuroplasticity. Embrace curiosity, seek out new challenges, and remain open to novel experiences. Every acquisition of knowledge and skill sets off a cascade of neural transformations, ensuring that your brain remains vibrant and adaptable throughout your journey.

Tapping into the power of neuroplasticity invites you to become the architect of your own mind. With deliberate intention, mindful practices, and a commitment to growth, harness the extraordinary potential within. As the neural symphony plays on, let the rhythm of neuroplasticity guide you toward a future sculpted by resilience, learning, and the limitless wonders of your evolving mind. Embrace the journey, for within it lies the transformative magic of self-discovery and unparalleled personal development.

The Role of Positive Affirmations and Visualization

In the landscape of personal transformation, positive affirmations and visualization emerge as potent tools, crafting the narrative of the reality we aspire to inhabit. Their influence goes beyond surface-level expressions; they serve as the architects shaping our mindset, manifesting our ambitions, and sculpting the life we yearn for.

Affirmations are not mere strings of words; they hold the transformative power to transmute self-doubt into confidence and fear into courage. By repeatedly affirming positive statements about ourselves and our goals, we sow the seeds of belief. These affirmations become incantations resonating with the core of our being, rewriting the script of our self-perception.

Cultivating an affirmative mindset becomes the focal point. Instead of fixating on limitations, positive affirmations redirect our attention to possibilities. They act as declarations of capabilities and visions of success, aligning the subconscious mind with these positive declarations and paving the way for tangible transformation.

Visualization complements this narrative by creating mental blueprints of our desired outcomes. It is the art of vividly painting mental images that serves as the foundation for the reality we aim to construct. By imaginatively experiencing our goals as already achieved, visualization becomes the compass guiding our actions and decisions toward manifestation.

Positive affirmations and visualization serve as tools to overcome self-imposed limitations. In the face of challenges, affirmations become declarations of resilience, while visualization acts as a mental rehearsal for triumph. Consistently reinforcing a positive narrative dismantles barriers that might hinder our progress.

These practices also contribute to the construction of a positive self-identity. By affirming our worth, capabilities, and potential, we redefine how we perceive ourselves. This reshaping of self-perception influences not only our behavior but also dictates the energy we emit into the world.

Affirmations and visualization create a magnetic energy that draws opportunities and abundance into our lives. As we consistently radiate positivity, we attract circumstances and people aligned with our aspirations. This magnetic force becomes the catalyst for the serendipities and synchronicities that propel us forward.

Incorporating positive affirmations and visualization into our daily rituals is a commitment to self-empowerment. Whether through morning mantras or evening reflections, these practices shape our mindset, setting the tone for the day and influencing our perceptions of challenges.

These tools are not standalone remedies but synergize with intentional action. Affirmations and visualization fuel the motivation and confidence needed to take steps toward our goals. When accompanied by purposeful effort, these practices become catalysts for transformative change.

In essence, positive affirmations and visualization transcend mere words and mental images; they are the keystones of a mindset sculpted for success. By consistently infusing our thoughts with positivity and painting the canvas of our minds with vibrant images of achievement, we unlock doors to extraordinary possibilities. Embrace the power of affirmations and visualization, for within them lies the transformative magic of self-belief and the manifestation of our wildest aspirations.

Anecdote Episode - 2

In the bustling city of Boston, April 15, 2013, was marked as the annual Boston Marathon, a day that traditionally celebrated athleticism, endurance, and community spirit. Runners from around the world gathered to participate in one of the oldest and most prestigious marathons. However, this particular day would be etched into history for a different reason: it became a day of tragedy and resilience.

As the marathon unfolded, the joyous atmosphere turned somber when two bombs exploded near the finish line on Boylston Street. The blasts resulted in a devastating act of terrorism, leaving three people dead and injuring hundreds more. Among the survivors was Adrianne Haslet, a vibrant and accomplished professional dancer.

Adrianne, at the time a dance instructor and performer, had been present near the finish line to cheer on the runners and soak in the celebratory atmosphere. The sudden and shocking turn of events left her severely injured, and she emerged from the chaos with the profound loss of her left leg below the knee.

Adrianne's journey to recovery was nothing short of extraordinary, showcasing the remarkable plasticity of the human mind. The initial shock and pain were overwhelming, but Adrianne's spirit refused to be broken. From the very beginning, she set her sights on reclaiming not just her mobility but also her passion for dance.

As Adrianne entered the world of rehabilitation, the concept of neuroplasticity took center stage. With a fierce determination, she began the arduous process of rewiring her brain to adapt to her new reality. The physical therapy sessions were grueling, but Adrianne embraced the challenges, seeing each hurdle as a step closer to the dance floor.

Throughout the rehabilitation process, Adrianne's mindset played a pivotal role. She refused to let the limitations of her prosthetic leg define her. Instead, she focused on what was possible and what she could achieve. Positive affirmations became her daily ritual, a mantra that echoed in her mind: "I am not just a survivor; I am a dancer, and nothing can take that away from me."

The turning point came when Adrianne decided to step back onto the dance floor. With a customized prosthetic leg designed for movement, she faced the mirror, her reflection a testament to resilience. The first tentative steps evolved into graceful movements as she danced to the rhythm of her own determination.

Adrianne's story became a beacon of inspiration, not just for amputees but for anyone facing adversity. She proved that the plasticity of the mind could triumph over physical limitations. Through her journey, Adrianne shattered preconceived notions of what was possible, showcasing the incredible adaptability of the human brain.

Her triumphant return to the stage was a moment of pure wonder. Adrianne not only performed but also became an advocate for amputee dancers, pushing boundaries and challenging stereotypes. Her unwavering spirit, combined with the science of neuroplasticity, allowed her to rewrite her story and redefine what it meant to dance against the odds.

Adrianne Haslet's journey reminds us that the wonders within our minds can overcome even the most challenging circumstances. Her story is a celebration of resilience, determination, and the limitless possibilities that unfold when the human spirit refuses to be confined by adversity.

Chapter 3

Embracing The Unknown

Stepping Beyond Comfort Zones

Embarking on the journey of personal growth often requires venturing into uncharted territories, away from the familiarity of our comfort zones. This process is not merely about seeking discomfort for its own sake but about acknowledging the transformative power that lies beyond the boundaries of what we know.

Comfort zones serve as protective bubbles, shielding us from the uncertainties and challenges that exist beyond their confines. However, growth and self-discovery thrive in realms that extend beyond the comfortable and familiar. Stepping into the unknown is a conscious decision to expand our horizons, confront our fears, and unlock the dormant potential that resides within.

The decision to step beyond comfort zones is an act of courage. It is an acknowledgment that real growth occurs when we are willing to embrace discomfort and face the uncertainties that accompany change. This journey demands a mindset shift—a willingness to trade the safety of the known for the excitement of the unknown.

Challenges and discomfort are not adversaries but rather companions on the path to self-realization. They are the catalysts that propel us out of stagnation and into a state of continuous evolution. The process of stepping beyond comfort zones is an invitation to reevaluate our perceived limitations, question self-imposed boundaries, and redefine what we believe is possible.

As we navigate the unexplored territories, we often discover facets of ourselves that remain hidden within the safety of our comfort zones. New skills are honed, resilience is forged, and a profound sense of self-efficacy emerges. Every step taken outside the familiar realm becomes a testament to our capacity for growth and adaptability.

The magic lies in the discomfort itself. It's a signal that we are pushing the boundaries of what we thought we could achieve. It's an acknowledgment that we are not settling for mediocrity but reaching for the extraordinary. Each moment of unease becomes a stepping stone toward a version of ourselves that is more resilient, capable, and aligned with our true potential.

The journey beyond comfort zones is not a linear path; it is a continuous cycle of exploration, adaptation, and growth. It involves embracing uncertainty, learning from failures, and celebrating successes. It is a testament to our willingness to evolve, to transcend the limitations we once accepted, and to chart a course toward a more expansive and fulfilling life.

In conclusion, stepping beyond comfort zones is an essential pilgrimage on the road to personal development. It is a conscious choice to challenge the status quo, embrace discomfort, and unlock the untapped reservoirs of potential that lie within. As we venture into the unknown, we not only discover the vast landscapes of our capabilities but also unveil the extraordinary possibilities that await us outside the confines of what is familiar and safe.

Finding Comfort in Uncertainty

In the ebb and flow of life, uncertainty stands as a constant companion, weaving its threads through the fabric of our existence. Rather than viewing uncertainty as an adversary to be feared, what if we could find comfort in its ever-changing nature? What if, in the midst of life's unpredictability, we could discover a sanctuary of resilience and growth?

Finding comfort in uncertainty is not an act of resignation but a profound shift in perspective—an acknowledgment that, within the nebulous realms of the unknown, lie opportunities for self-discovery and transformation.

At the heart of this shift is the understanding that certainty is an illusion. The very nature of life is dynamic, filled with twists and turns that challenge our expectations. Rather than resisting this inherent unpredictability, we can choose to embrace it as the fertile ground from which resilience and adaptability sprout.

Consider uncertainty as the canvas upon which the masterpiece of your life unfolds. In the absence of rigid expectations, the brushstrokes of possibility become more vivid. It is within this uncertainty that the palette of opportunities is vast and varied, waiting for you to create your unique painting.

The pursuit of certainty often leads to stagnation—a resistance to change that hinders personal growth.

In contrast, finding comfort in uncertainty propels us forward. It's an invitation to dance with the unknown, to navigate uncharted waters with the confidence that even in uncertainty, there exists a rhythm that can be embraced.

Adopting a mindset that sees uncertainty as a catalyst for growth transforms the way we approach challenges. Instead of viewing obstacles as insurmountable barriers, we recognize them as stepping stones toward self-improvement. Every twist and turn becomes an opportunity to test our resilience, adaptability, and resourcefulness.

In the space of uncertainty, we discover the beauty of impermanence. Life's transient nature invites us to savor the present moment, appreciating the richness it offers. When we release the need for absolute control, we open ourselves to the serendipities that arise in the spontaneity of the uncertain journey.

The journey of finding comfort in uncertainty is not a one-time endeavor but a continuous practice. It involves cultivating self-awareness, building resilience, and nurturing a mindset that thrives amid life's fluctuations. As we navigate the unknown, we not only find comfort but also unveil the hidden potentials that lie within us.

In conclusion, finding comfort in uncertainty is a transformative choice—one that shifts our perception from fear to curiosity, from resistance to acceptance. It's a journey of self-discovery and resilience, where we learn to dance with the uncertainties of life, finding solace in the knowledge that within the unknown, there exists a canvas of endless possibilities waiting to be explored and embraced.

The Magic That Happens Outside Familiar Territories

In the vast expanse of our comfort zones, where the familiar and routine provide a sense of security, lies an invitation to explore the uncharted territories that hold the promise of magic and transformation. Beyond the boundaries of what we know, outside the realms of familiarity, is where the true alchemy of self-discovery occurs.

The magic that happens outside familiar territories is not just a departure from routine; it's an immersion into the extraordinary possibilities that exist beyond the confines of what we consider safe. It's a journey that beckons us to venture into the unknown, to step outside the well-trodden paths and to embrace the richness that lies in unexplored landscapes.

Consider your comfort zone as a cocoon—a place of safety and routine. While it provides a sense of security, it is in breaking free from this cocoon that the wings of potential unfold. The magic begins when we dare to stretch our boundaries and acknowledge that growth and transformation thrive in the unexplored territories outside our habitual existence.

The unfamiliar can be intimidating, but it is also where resilience is forged. It is in the face of challenges and uncertainties that we discover the depth of our capabilities. Every step taken beyond the familiar becomes a catalyst for personal evolution, an opportunity to unveil the latent powers that reside within.

Magic unfolds when we relinquish the need for absolute control. The unknown is not a realm to be feared but a canvas awaiting the strokes of our courage and curiosity. It's in the dance with uncertainty that we find the rhythm of resilience and adaptability, qualities that are essential for navigating the ever-changing landscape of life.

The magic outside familiar territories lies in the serendipities that unfold when we embrace the unexpected. It's in the connections made, the lessons learned, and the experiences that challenge our perspectives. The richness of life expands when we allow ourselves to be open to the diverse and unexpected gifts that unexplored territories bring.

The journey outside the familiar is not without discomfort, but it is within this discomfort that the seeds of growth are sown. The challenges encountered become stepping stones to a version of ourselves that is more robust, more capable, and more attuned to the wonders that life has to offer.

In conclusion, the magic that happens outside familiar territories is an invitation to embark on a transformative journey—a journey where the ordinary transforms into the extraordinary. It's a conscious choice to explore the uncharted, to dance with uncertainty, and to embrace the richness of life. As we step into the unknown, we not only discover the magic that lies outside the familiar but also unfold the chapters of a story filled with resilience, growth, and the limitless possibilities that await us.

Anecdote Episode - 3

In the picturesque Swat Valley of Pakistan, where the mountains echoed with stories of resilience, a young girl named Malala Yousafzai emerged as a symbol of unwavering courage and an advocate for education. Malala's story unfolded against the backdrop of a region grappling with the oppressive rule of the Taliban, who sought to silence the voices that dared to challenge their dogma.

Malala was born in Mingora, Swat, in 1997, into a family that valued education. Her father, Ziauddin Yousafzai, ran a school, instilling in Malala a deep appreciation for the transformative power of learning. As the Taliban's influence grew, so did their restrictions on education, particularly for girls. Undeterred, Malala became a voice for the voiceless, an eloquent advocate for the right to education.

The turning point came in 2009 when Malala began writing a blog for the BBC Urdu under a pseudonym, detailing her life under Taliban rule and the challenges faced by girls who aspired to learn. Her eloquent words and unyielding determination caught the world's attention, earning her the prestigious National Youth Peace Prize in Pakistan.

As Malala's prominence grew, so did the threats from the Taliban. In October 2012, a fateful day on her school bus, she was shot in the head by a Taliban gunman. The world watched in horror as a young girl's pursuit of education became a symbol of resistance against oppression.

Miraculously surviving the attack, Malala's resolve only strengthened. Recovering in the United Kingdom, she continued her advocacy for education, delivering impassioned speeches at international forums. In 2014, at the age of 17, Malala became the youngest-ever recipient of the Nobel Peace Prize, alongside Kailash Satyarthi, for their struggle against the suppression of children and young people and for the right of all children to education.

Malala's educational crusade transcended cultural boundaries, inspiring millions globally to stand up for the right to education. She co-authored the memoir "I Am Malala: The Girl Who Stood Up for Education and Was Shot by the Taliban," providing a firsthand account of her journey and the importance of education in the face of adversity.

Malala's story embodies the essence of embracing the unknown. She stepped beyond the comfort of silence, found solace in uncertainty, and navigated unfamiliar territories to champion a cause that went beyond personal safety. The magic in her story lies in the transformative impact of education on individuals and communities, proving that the pen, indeed, can be mightier than the sword.

Today, Malala continues to advocate for education through the Malala Fund, amplifying her message that every girl has the right to twelve years of free, safe, and quality education. Her story remains an enduring testament to the resilience of the human spirit and the profound magic that unfolds when one dares to embrace the unknown for the greater good.

Chapter 4

The Art of Transformative Thinking

Mastering the Mind-Shift

In the intricate mosaic of personal development, there exists a potent catalyst that transcends the realms of strategy and technique. It's the master key that unlocks doors to resilience, innovation, and transformative growth—this key is the art of mastering the mind shift.

At its core, mastering the mind shift is not a mere change in perception; it's a profound rewiring of the cognitive pathways that govern our thoughts, beliefs, and reactions. It's a deliberate choice to sculpt a mindset that fosters adaptability, resilience, and a relentless pursuit of growth.

The foundation of this transformative journey lies in our understanding of the power inherent in our thoughts. Our minds are not passive observers but active architects, shaping the reality we experience. Mastering the mind shift requires a vigilant awareness of our thought patterns, allowing us to intercept and redirect them toward positive and empowering narratives.

One of the pivotal aspects of this shift is embracing the concept of a growth mindset. Rather than viewing abilities as fixed traits, a growth mindset sees challenges as opportunities for learning and improvement. It's an understanding that talents can be developed through dedication and hard work, laying the groundwork for a journey of continuous evolution.

The art of mastering the mind shift involves a conscious choice to view setbacks not as failures but as stepping stones toward success. Instead of being paralyzed by fear of failure, individuals who have mastered the mind-shift use setbacks as valuable feedback, adjusting their approach and forging ahead with renewed determination.

Resilience becomes a cornerstone of this transformative journey. It's the ability to bounce back from adversity, viewing obstacles not as insurmountable barriers but as temporary hurdles. Mastering the mind shift cultivates resilience by reframing challenges as opportunities for personal and professional growth.

In the realm of innovation and creativity, mastering the mind shift enables individuals to break free from the constraints of conventional thinking. It's an invitation to explore new perspectives, challenge assumptions, and embrace the discomfort that often accompanies uncharted territory. The mind-shifted individual becomes an architect of innovative solutions, unafraid to venture beyond the familiar.

The transformative power of mastering the mind shift extends to the realm of self-belief. It involves silencing the inner critic and fostering a mindset that believes in one's capabilities. By cultivating self-confidence and acknowledging one's worth, individuals can navigate challenges with a steadfast determination to overcome obstacles.

Ultimately, mastering the mind shift is an ongoing journey—one that requires commitment, self-reflection, and a willingness to challenge ingrained thought patterns. It's a journey that transcends the boundaries of circumstance, empowering individuals to navigate the complexities of life with grace, resilience, and an unwavering belief in their ability to overcome and thrive.

In conclusion, the art of mastering the mind-shift is a transformative expedition into the very core of our being. It's a journey that empowers us to wield the immense power of our thoughts, cultivate resilience in the face of adversity, and embrace a growth mindset that propels us toward continuous evolution. As we master the mind shift, we unlock the door to a future brimming with possibilities—a future where our thoughts shape the reality of our extraordinary potential.

Overcoming Limiting Beliefs Through Cognitive Restructuring

In the labyrinth of personal development, one formidable adversary often lurks in the shadows—the limiting beliefs that whisper doubts about our abilities, potential, and worthiness. Yet, within the vast landscape of the mind, there exists a powerful tool for dismantling these self-imposed barriers—cognitive restructuring.

Cognitive restructuring is not a mere rearrangement of thoughts; it's a profound transformation of the mental landscape. It's the deliberate act of challenging and reshaping the beliefs that constrict our potential, replacing them with empowering narratives that propel us toward growth and self-actualization.

At the heart of cognitive restructuring lies the recognition that beliefs are not absolute truths but interpretations shaped by experiences, perceptions, and conditioning. By cultivating a heightened awareness of our thought patterns, we gain the ability to intercept and redirect these limiting beliefs, opening the door to a world of boundless possibilities.

The first step in this transformative journey is the identification of limiting beliefs. These are the subtle whispers that echo in moments of self-doubt, the narratives that cast shadows on our aspirations. Once identified, the process of cognitive restructuring involves questioning the validity of these beliefs and challenging the evidence that supports them.

A key component of cognitive restructuring is embracing the power of positive affirmations. By consciously replacing negative self-talk with affirmations that reinforce our capabilities and worth, we begin to sow the seeds of a more empowering belief system. The repetition of these affirmations serves as a steady drip of positivity, gradually eroding the foundations of limiting beliefs.

An integral aspect of dismantling limiting beliefs is reframing failures and setbacks. Rather than viewing them as confirmations of inadequacy, cognitive restructuring invites us to see them as opportunities for growth and learning. Failures become stepping stones; each misstep is a lesson that propels us toward mastery and resilience.

The process of cognitive restructuring is not a one-time endeavor but a continuous practice. It requires a commitment to self-reflection, a willingness to challenge ingrained thought patterns, and the patience to replace limiting beliefs with affirming truths. This journey is a gradual unfurling, a blossoming of the mind toward a more expansive and empowering understanding of oneself.

As limiting beliefs crumble under the weight of cognitive restructuring, individuals experience a profound shift in their perception of themselves and their capabilities. Confidence emerges from the ashes of self-doubt, and a renewed sense of agency takes root. The individual becomes the architect of their narrative, rewriting the script of their life with chapters of empowerment and resilience.

In conclusion, overcoming limiting beliefs through cognitive restructuring is a transformative odyssey into the recesses of the mind. It's a journey that empowers us to challenge the narratives that hinder our growth, replacing them with affirming truths that resonate with our highest potential. As we navigate this inner landscape, we discover that the keys to unlocking our true capabilities have been within us all along, waiting to be unearthed through the profound alchemy of cognitive restructuring.

How Positive Thinking Can Catapult You to Wondrous Heights

In the kaleidoscope of personal development, one lens holds a transformative power that extends far beyond mere optimism—it's the profound influence of positive thinking. Far from being a simplistic mantra, positive thinking is a dynamic force that can catapult individuals to wondrous heights, reshaping their realities and propelling them toward unprecedented achievements.

At its essence, positive thinking is not about wearing rose-colored glasses that blur the complexities of life; rather, it's a conscious choice to focus on the constructive and optimistic facets of situations. It is a mindset that cultivates hope, resilience, and a belief in the possibility of favorable outcomes even in the face of challenges.

The impact of positive thinking on individual trajectories is profound. It acts as a catalyst for resilience, infusing individuals with the strength to navigate turbulent waters. When faced with setbacks, those embracing positive thinking perceive them not as insurmountable obstacles but as opportunities for growth and learning.

One of the remarkable facets of positive thinking lies in its ability to shape the narrative individuals tell themselves. The stories we internalize about our capabilities and the world around us influence our actions and reactions. Positive thinking empowers individuals to rewrite these narratives, fostering self-belief and confidence in their ability to overcome adversity.

The transformative power of positive thinking extends to the realm of goal-setting and achievement. When individuals approach their aspirations with a positive mindset, they are more likely to persevere in the face of challenges, maintain focus, and adapt to changing circumstances. Their optimistic energy becomes a driving force that propels them toward the realization of their dreams.

Moreover, positive thinking is not a passive state of mind; it's an active engagement with the present moment. It involves a deliberate choice to redirect thoughts from dwelling on limitations to envisioning possibilities. In this process, individuals become architects of their realities, shaping a future infused with the vibrancy of their positive perspectives.

The impact of positive thinking is not limited to individual well-being; it radiates outward, influencing the environments individuals inhabit. Positivity is contagious, fostering a ripple effect that uplifts not only the individual but also those around them. In cultivating a positive mindset, individuals contribute to the creation of a supportive and optimistic community.

In conclusion, the journey fueled by positive thinking is a transformative odyssey into the limitless possibilities of the human psyche. It is a dynamic force that propels individuals to wondrous heights by instilling resilience, shaping empowering narratives, and fostering a belief in the extraordinary potential within. As individuals embrace positive thinking, they unearth the keys to unlocking their true capabilities, and in doing so, they catapult themselves to heights that were once deemed unattainable.

Anecdote Episode - 4

In the vibrant city of Rameswaram, nestled along the southern coast of India, a young boy named Avul Pakir Jainulabdeen Abdul Kalam dreamt of the skies. Little did the world know that this boy, born into a humble family, would one day soar to unimaginable heights and become the architect of a vision that aimed to transform India.

Abdul Kalam's journey began against the backdrop of post-independence India, grappling with numerous challenges. Born in 1931, he witnessed the struggles of a newly formed nation striving for socio-economic development. Kalam's fascination with flight and space fueled his educational pursuits, leading him to study aeronautical engineering and ultimately contribute significantly to India's space and missile programs.

However, it was not just technological advancements that fueled Abdul Kalam's vision. His transformative thinking extended beyond the realm of science and technology to encompass the socio-economic fabric of the nation. In 2002, when he assumed the role of the 11th President of India, he articulated a vision for the country—a vision of a "developed India by 2020."

This vision wasn't merely a set of lofty goals; it was a call to action that resonated with millions. Dr. Kalam believed in the power of education as the cornerstone of societal transformation. He emphasized the need for India to harness the potential of its youth, envisioning a nation where knowledge and innovation would be the driving forces of progress.

Throughout his presidency, Dr. Kalam tirelessly advocated for education, particularly in the fields of science and technology. He visited schools and universities, engaging with students and encouraging them to dream big. His speeches, often peppered with anecdotes from his own life, inspired a generation to overcome obstacles, think innovatively, and contribute to the nation's growth.

One of Dr. Kalam's key messages was the importance of self-reliance. He believed that a transformed India could only be achieved when the nation reduced dependence on external sources and harnessed its own capabilities. This vision echoed in his interactions with scientists, policymakers, and common citizens, urging everyone to play a role in the journey towards a developed nation.

Dr. Kalam's transformative thinking went hand in hand with his humility and accessibility. Often referred to as the "People's President," he remained deeply connected with the masses, making science and technology accessible and relatable. His ability to communicate complex ideas in a simple and inspiring manner endeared him to people of all ages and backgrounds.

The vision set forth by A.P.J. Abdul Kalam began to materialize as India made significant strides in various fields. The nation embraced technological advancements, witnessed economic growth, and saw a burgeoning youth population eager to contribute to the country's development.

Although Dr. Kalam's term as president concluded in 2007, his vision continued to guide the nation even after his departure. His legacy lives on in initiatives like the "National Action Plan for Climate Change" and "PURA" (Providing Urban Amenities in Rural Areas), reflecting his commitment to inclusive and sustainable development.

A.P.J. Abdul Kalam's vision for a transformed India was not merely a goal but a collective aspiration. His story is a testament to the transformative power of visionary thinking, reinforcing the notion that by embracing the unknown, stepping beyond comfort zones, and cultivating a positive mindset, individuals and nations alike can achieve wondrous heights.

Chapter 5

The Wonder of Resilience

Building Mental Toughness for Endurance

In the arena of personal development, where the journey often demands resilience and unwavering perseverance, the concept of building mental toughness emerges as a formidable ally. It goes beyond physical endurance, delving into the realms of the mind and forging a tenacious spirit capable of withstanding the trials of life's marathon.

Mental toughness is not an innate trait reserved for a select few; rather, it is a skill that can be honed and cultivated through deliberate practice and mindset shifts. At its core, it is the ability to remain focused, composed, and determined in the face of adversity, creating a reservoir of inner strength that propels individuals through challenges and setbacks.

The foundation of building mental toughness lies in cultivating a resilient mindset. It's an understanding that setbacks and obstacles are not roadblocks but rather stepping stones toward growth. Individuals with mental toughness view challenges as opportunities to test their mettle, learn valuable lessons, and emerge stronger on the other side.

A crucial aspect of mental toughness is the development of a positive self-talk mechanism. The inner dialogue we engage in during challenging moments significantly influences our ability to endure. Cultivating a positive and empowering self-talk habit involves consciously replacing negative thoughts with affirmations of resilience, capability, and determination.

The journey of building mental toughness also entails embracing discomfort. Endurance, in its truest form, requires navigating through discomfort with steadfast resolve. This involves pushing beyond perceived limits, whether physical or mental, and learning to thrive in the discomfort that often precedes growth.

A key component of mental toughness is adaptability. Life's journey is unpredictable, and mental toughness equips individuals with the ability to adapt to changing circumstances. Rather than being paralyzed by unexpected challenges, those with mental toughness recalibrate their approach, finding innovative solutions and forging ahead.

Visualizing success becomes a powerful tool in the arsenal of mental toughness. The ability to vividly imagine triumphs and achievements serves as a mental rehearsal, preparing individuals for the challenges they may face. Visualization becomes a compass that guides their actions and decisions, aligning them with the path toward enduring success.

Moreover, building mental toughness involves embracing a growth mindset. Rather than viewing abilities as fixed, individuals with mental toughness approach challenges with the belief that skills can be developed through dedication and effort. This mindset fosters a hunger for continuous improvement and fuels the resilience needed for enduring challenges.

In conclusion, the journey of building mental toughness is an expedition into the depths of one's character. It is a deliberate cultivation of resilience, adaptability, and a relentless spirit that can endure life's endurance tests. As individuals fortify their mental toughness, they emerge not only as survivors but as victors, capable of navigating the twists and turns of life's marathon with grace, determination, and an unyielding spirit that stands the test of time.

Turning Adversity into a Launchpad for Success

In the crucible of life, adversity stands as an inevitable force, capable of shaking the foundations of our resolve. Yet, within the chaos of challenges and setbacks lies a transformative opportunity—to turn adversity into a launchpad for success.

Adversity is not a signal to surrender; it's a call to rise. It beckons individuals to harness the transformative power embedded in every obstacle, to turn setbacks into stepping stones, and to sculpt success from the raw material of adversity.

The first step in this transformative journey is a shift in perspective. Rather than viewing adversity as an insurmountable barrier, individuals who turn adversity into a launchpad perceive it as a crucible for growth. It becomes the raw material for resilience, innovation, and a steely determination to carve a path toward success.

Embracing adversity requires a resilient mindset—an unwavering belief that challenges are not roadblocks but opportunities for learning and refinement. It's a commitment to face difficulties head-on, understanding that each trial is a test of character and a potential catalyst for personal and professional evolution.

Within the heart of adversity lies the power of choice. Individuals can choose how they respond to challenges. Instead of succumbing to despair, those who turn adversity into a launchpad make a conscious decision to respond with courage, creativity, and an indomitable spirit. Adversity becomes a canvas upon which they paint their tales of resilience.

The transformative journey involves extracting lessons from adversity. Every setback and every failure becomes a source of valuable insights. Rather than viewing these experiences as defeats, individuals use them as data points, refining their strategies and fine-tuning their approaches on the path to success.

Moreover, turning adversity into a launchpad involves cultivating adaptability. Life is inherently unpredictable, and the ability to adapt to unforeseen circumstances is a hallmark of success. Adversity becomes a training ground for adaptability, a crucible that tempers individuals into agile navigators of life's tumultuous seas.

In the realm of personal development, the process of turning adversity into a launchpad is synonymous with resilience. Resilient individuals do not crumble in the face of adversity; they bounce back with renewed vigor. Adversity becomes the forge that shapes their inner strength, enabling them to withstand the storms and emerge stronger on the other side.

In conclusion, turning adversity into a launchpad is a transformative choice—a commitment to extracting strength, wisdom, and innovation from life's challenges. It is a journey that requires resilience, adaptability, and a mindset that views adversity not as a roadblock but as a springboard toward success. As individuals embrace this perspective, they unlock the latent potential within adversity, turning each setback into a launching point for a future adorned with triumphs, growth, and extraordinary success born from the crucible of challenges.

The Surprising Benefits of Embracing Challenges

In the journey of personal growth, challenges stand as both inevitable obstacles and unexpected allies. Instead of viewing challenges as adversaries to be avoided, what if we could recognize them as catalysts for profound transformation? The surprising benefits of embracing challenges extend beyond mere resilience; they shape our character, fortify our spirit, and pave the way for unparalleled personal and professional growth.

One of the surprising benefits lies in the revelation of untapped strengths. Challenges have a remarkable ability to unearth dormant capabilities within us. When faced with adversity, we often discover reservoirs of resilience, creativity, and determination that may have remained concealed in the absence of tribulations. Embracing challenges becomes an exploration of our untapped potential.

Embracing challenges is also a powerful teacher of adaptability. Life is dynamic, and the ability to adapt to changing circumstances is a skill of immeasurable value. Challenges, with their ever-shifting nature, provide a training ground for adaptability. Through each trial, we learn to navigate the unpredictable currents of life, emerging not only unscathed but more adept at charting our course.

Moreover, challenges are catalysts for innovation and creativity. When confronted with obstacles, our minds are stirred into finding novel solutions. The necessity of overcoming challenges compels us to think beyond the conventional, fostering a mindset of innovation. In the crucible of challenges, we become architects of inventive solutions that often surpass our initial expectations.

Embracing challenges is a forge for resilience. Just as a blacksmith tempers metal in the fire to strengthen it, challenges temper our character. Through adversity, we develop the resilience needed to bounce back from setbacks, face uncertainties with courage, and persevere in the pursuit of our goals. Resilience becomes the bedrock upon which we build our enduring success.

The surprising benefits of challenges extend to personal growth. Challenges invite self-reflection and self-discovery. In navigating obstacles, we gain insights into our values, priorities, and aspirations. Challenges become mirrors, reflecting not only the external hurdles but also the internal landscapes waiting to be explored and understood.

Furthermore, embracing challenges fosters a growth mindset. Rather than seeing challenges as insurmountable roadblocks, individuals with a growth mindset perceive them as opportunities for learning and improvement. Challenges become stepping stones toward personal and professional development, propelling us forward on the journey of continuous growth.

In conclusion, the surprising benefits of embracing challenges lie in the profound transformation they bring to our lives. Challenges are not adversaries to be feared but allies that sculpt our character, unveil our strengths, and propel us toward unparalleled growth. As we welcome challenges with an open heart and a resilient spirit, we discover that each obstacle carries the potential for extraordinary benefits—an unexpected gift on the path to becoming the architects of our destiny.

Anecdote Episode - 5

Born on February 8, 1990, on the island paradise renowned for its breathtaking landscapes and vibrant surfing culture, Bethany's connection to the sea was woven into the fabric of her upbringing. Growing up in a family of avid surfers, Bethany was introduced to the art of riding waves at an early age. Kauai, with its pristine beaches and world-class surf breaks, provided the perfect backdrop for her to cultivate a deep and unbreakable bond with the ocean. From the gentle swells to the challenging reef breaks, Bethany embraced the waves as a playground where she felt a sense of freedom, exhilaration, and a profound connection to nature.

Her childhood in Kauai was infused with the spirit of aloha, a cultural ethos emphasizing love, compassion, and living in harmony with the land and sea. Bethany's days were spent chasing the sunsets, paddling into the crystal-clear waters, and honing her surfing skills under the golden Hawaiian sun. The waves, with their soothing melody, became the soundtrack of her youth and the canvas upon which she painted her dreams.

In this idyllic island setting, Bethany's passion for surfing blossomed into a love affair with the ocean's energy. Kauai's surf culture, characterized by a tight-knit community of surfers, encouraged her to push her limits and embrace the thrill of catching waves. Little did she know that the very waves she loved would become the backdrop to a story of extraordinary resilience that would unfold in the years to come.

The fateful morning of October 31, 2003, began like any other for Bethany. As she paddled into the azure waters, a sudden encounter with a tiger shark changed her life forever. In the midst of the attack, Bethany's left arm was severed, leaving her in a battle for her life. Miraculously, she survived, emerging from the ocean with an unyielding spirit that would become the hallmark of her extraordinary journey.

Bethany's return to the waves was nothing short of a triumph over adversity. Driven by an innate love for surfing, she refused to let the loss of her arm define her. With unwavering determination and the support of her family, Bethany embarked on a courageous journey to not only surf again but to compete at the professional level.

Her mental toughness and resilience shone through as she relearned the dynamics of surfing with a single arm. Through countless hours of practice, falls, and the occasional frustration, Bethany adapted her technique, mastering the art of balance and riding the waves with a grace that defied the odds. Her journey became a beacon of inspiration, captured in the film "Soul Surfer" and her autobiography of the same name.

"Soul Surfer" documented Bethany's physical and emotional struggles, laying bare the challenges she faced in returning to competitive surfing. Her story revealed the surprising benefits of embracing challenges, demonstrating that adversity could be a launchpad for success rather than a roadblock. Bethany's resilience became a powerful testament to the human spirit's capacity to transcend limitations.

As Bethany Hamilton returned to professional surfing, she didn't just participate; she excelled. Her triumphs in competitions and her fearlessness in the face of daunting waves showcased not only her surfing prowess but also the wonder of resilience. She became an icon of strength, inspiring individuals worldwide to overcome their own challenges with grace and determination.

Beyond the competitive arena, Bethany dedicated herself to empowering others. Through her foundation, she reached out to amputees and individuals facing adversity, showing them that they, too, could defy expectations. Her journey served as a reminder that the true measure of greatness lies not in avoiding challenges but in embracing them with an unbroken spirit.

Bethany Hamilton's story continues to resonate, echoing the power of resilience, mental toughness, and the surprising benefits that emerge from embracing challenges. Her remarkable journey inspires individuals to ride the waves of life with courage, to face adversity head-on, and to discover the greatness that lies within, waiting to be unleashed against the tide.

Chapter 6

The Wonder of Habits

Leveraging the Power of Positive Habits

In the symphony of personal development, the melody of success often emanates from the harmonious rhythm of positive habits. These seemingly mundane, daily practices possess a transformative power that extends far beyond routine—they are the architects of lasting change, the silent force that propels individuals toward their goals and aspirations.

At the core of leveraging the power of positive habits lies the understanding that small, consistent actions compound over time to yield significant results. It's a recognition that success is not solely the outcome of grand gestures but is, instead, an accumulation of the choices we make day in and day out.

Positive habits serve as the scaffolding upon which the architecture of success is built. They provide structure, routine, and a sense of discipline that is essential for navigating the complexities of life. By embedding positive habits into our daily lives, we create a framework that supports our aspirations and propels us toward our desired outcomes.

Moreover, positive habits act as catalysts for personal growth. They become the vehicle through which individuals continually evolve and refine themselves. Each positive habit is a commitment to self-improvement, a pledge to become a better version of the person we were yesterday. As these habits take root, they shape the trajectory of our character and contribute to the ongoing narrative of our development.

The power of positive habits lies in their ability to transcend motivation. While motivation may ebb and flow, positive habits function as steadfast companions that persist even when enthusiasm wanes. They provide a reliable structure that carries individuals through the inevitable fluctuations of motivation, ensuring progress is sustained even during challenging times.

Leveraging the power of positive habits involves making intentional choices. It's a conscious decision to cultivate habits that align with our goals and values. By carefully selecting habits that contribute to our well-being, personal development, and productivity, we design a lifestyle that propels us toward success.

Positive habits also influence the mindset. The act of consistently engaging in positive habits fosters a mindset of discipline, resilience, and self-efficacy. As individuals witness the impact of their daily practices, a belief in their ability to effect change is reinforced, creating a self-perpetuating cycle of success.

In conclusion, leveraging the power of positive habits is not merely about routine; it is a profound commitment to self-mastery and success. These habits are the architects of a life well lived—the keys to unlocking our fullest potential.

As we embrace and nurture positive habits, we embark on a transformative journey, sculpting the contours of a future defined by purpose, growth, and the extraordinary impact of daily, intentional choices.

Breaking Free from Destructive Patterns

In the vast landscape of personal growth, there exists a profound and empowering journey—the journey of breaking free from destructive patterns that have long held individuals captive. It's a transformative odyssey marked by courage, resilience, and a relentless pursuit of a life untethered from the chains of self-sabotage. Breaking free is not just an act of liberation; it is a declaration of self-worth, a commitment to change, and a celebration of the incredible strength residing within each person.

The first step on this transformative path is the courageous recognition of destructive patterns. It requires fearless introspection and an honest confrontation with the habits, thoughts, and behaviors that have hindered progress and the realization of one's full potential. This acknowledgment is not a sign of weakness; rather, it is a testament to the strength needed to face uncomfortable truths and choose a different path.

Breaking free from destructive patterns is, at its core, a shift in mindset. It involves challenging limiting beliefs that have perpetuated negative cycles. The realization that these patterns are learned responses, not inherent characteristics, becomes the seed from which a mindset of growth and self-empowerment can sprout. It is a conscious decision to rewrite the narrative that has dictated one's story thus far.

This transformative journey requires self-compassion—a gentle understanding that change is a process, not an instant destination. Setbacks are a natural part of the path, and self-compassion becomes the guiding light during moments of struggle. Embracing oneself with kindness and forgiveness reinforces the commitment to change and fuels the resilience needed for the journey ahead.

Breaking free also involves replacing destructive patterns with constructive alternatives. It's a deliberate choice to replace self-criticism with self-compassion, toxic habits with nurturing ones, and negative thought patterns with positive affirmations. Each intentional shift contributes to the creation of a new, empowering narrative—a narrative aligned with the vision of a life free from the constraints of destructive cycles.

The journey is not meant to be undertaken alone. Seeking support from mentors, therapists, or a supportive community can provide invaluable guidance and encouragement. The shared experiences of others who have embarked on similar journeys become beacons of inspiration, illuminating the way forward and reminding individuals that they are not alone in their quest for change.

In conclusion, breaking free from destructive patterns is a courageous act of self-liberation. It is a journey that transcends limitations, shatters self-imposed barriers, and unveils the remarkable strength within. As individuals embark on this transformative odyssey, they embrace a future defined by empowerment, resilience, and the boundless possibilities that arise when they courageously choose to break free from the patterns that no longer serve them.

Creating a Lifestyle That Fosters Continuous Growth

In the journey of personal development, the creation of a lifestyle that fosters continuous growth stands as a masterpiece—a living testament to the unwavering commitment to evolve, learn, and become the best version of oneself. It's not just about setting goals or achieving milestones; it's a holistic approach that transforms every facet of life into a canvas for perpetual self-improvement.

At the core of a growth-oriented lifestyle lies a mindset that hungers for knowledge and embraces challenges. It's a mindset that sees every experience, positive or negative, as an opportunity for learning and growth. Instead of viewing setbacks as failures, individuals on this path perceive them as stepping stones toward mastery and resilience.

Continuous growth is cultivated through intentional choices—choices that prioritize self-care, nourishment, and mental well-being. It involves a commitment to regular exercise, a balanced diet, and adequate sleep. The body, mind, and spirit are interconnected, and nurturing each aspect contributes to an environment where growth can flourish.

A growth-oriented lifestyle involves the conscious pursuit of new skills and knowledge. Whether through formal education, self-directed learning, or experiential endeavors, the commitment to acquiring and applying knowledge becomes a perpetual journey. It's an understanding that growth is not a destination but a lifelong expedition.

Moreover, a lifestyle of continuous growth is grounded in self-reflection. It requires the willingness to reflect, evaluate one's values and priorities, and adjust course when needed. Through self-reflection, individuals gain insights into their strengths, areas for improvement, and the values that guide their journey toward continuous growth.

Embracing challenges becomes a cornerstone of a growth-oriented lifestyle. Challenges are not avoided but embraced as opportunities for expansion. Rather than seeking comfort in the familiar, individuals on this path deliberately step into the discomfort of the unknown, recognizing that it is within challenges that the seeds of growth are sown.

Connection and collaboration are integral components of a growth-oriented lifestyle. Engaging with a community that shares similar values fosters inspiration, support, and accountability. The exchange of ideas, experiences, and encouragement becomes a dynamic force propelling individuals forward on their journey of continuous growth.

In conclusion, creating a lifestyle that fosters continuous growth is a profound commitment to the ongoing evolution of self. It's a journey that transcends the confines of routine and familiarity, inviting individuals to embrace a mindset of curiosity, resilience, and perpetual improvement. As each day unfolds and intentional choices are made in alignment with growth, individuals craft a life that is not just lived but continually transformed—a life brimming with the richness of learning, resilience, and the limitless potential that comes from embracing the journey of continuous growth.

Anecdote Episode - 6

In the bustling city of Kolkata, against the backdrop of post-independence India, a man with an unyielding spirit and a dedication to disciplined living emerged as a beacon of inspiration. Born in 1912, Manohar Aich's life unfolded against the canvas of a world in flux. 1912 marked the end of an era in India, as it was the year before the outbreak of World War I. His birth year placed him on the cusp of significant historical events, setting the stage for a life that would unfold as a testament to resilience, discipline, and the transformative power of positive habits.

As Aich grew, so did the fervor for independence in India. The 1920s and 1930s witnessed the rise of the independence movement, with pivotal events such as the Non-Cooperation Movement and the Civil Disobedience Movement shaping the nation's destiny. He, coming of age during these transformative years, would have been witness to the evolving socio-political landscape and the burgeoning spirit of freedom that swept across the subcontinent.

By the time Aich entered adulthood, the stage was set for momentous changes. The 1940s saw the intensification of the struggle for independence, marked by the Quit India Movement and the eventual attainment of freedom in 1947. Against this backdrop of political upheaval and the birth of a newly independent India, Aich's personal journey began to intertwine with the collective aspirations of a nation.

Amidst the challenges and triumphs of post-independence India, Aich's commitment to physical fitness and disciplined living emerged as a guiding light. The transformative power of positive habits became the cornerstone of his life, shaping not only his personal achievements but also contributing to a broader narrative of self-improvement and resilience.

Manohar Aich's journey into the world of bodybuilding was far from conventional. Standing at a modest 4 feet 11 inches, he faced physical challenges that might have deterred others. However, Aich's determination knew no bounds. In the early 1940s, he entered the realm of bodybuilding, driven by an innate passion for fitness and an unwavering belief in the power of disciplined living.

One of the defining aspects of Manohar Aich's story was his commitment to positive habits and a structured lifestyle. His day began with the rising sun as he engaged in rigorous physical exercises on the banks of the Hooghly River. Aich embraced a holistic approach to fitness, combining traditional Indian exercises with Western bodybuilding techniques. His disciplined routine included not only weightlifting but also yoga, calisthenics, and a balanced diet.

The transformative power of Aich's positive habits became evident as he swiftly rose through the ranks of bodybuilding competitions in India. In 1950, he claimed the title of Mr. Hercules, marking the beginning of a remarkable journey. However, Aich's ultimate triumph came in 1952, when he secured the coveted title of Mr. Universe, becoming the first Indian to achieve this prestigious honor.

Beyond the glitz and glamor of the bodybuilding stage, Manohar Aich's story held profound lessons in discipline, perseverance, and the wonders of cultivating positive habits. His commitment to fitness was not just about sculpting his own physique; it was a testament to the transformative impact that intentional routines and disciplined living can have on an individual's life.

In the face of financial constraints and the challenges of a post-colonial India, Aich's discipline extended beyond the gym. He balanced a full-time job with his passion for bodybuilding, showcasing an extraordinary work ethic.

His story became a source of inspiration for countless individuals, proving that with dedication and positive habits, one could overcome physical limitations and achieve greatness.

Manohar Aich's legacy continued well into his later years, as he remained an advocate for a healthy lifestyle. Even in his 90s, he maintained a disciplined routine, continuing to inspire generations. His story remains etched in the annals of Indian sports history, not only for his accolades in bodybuilding but also for the enduring impact of his disciplined approach to life.

The iron disciple, as Manohar Aich came to be known, demonstrated that the wonder of habits goes beyond the physical realm. It is a philosophy of life, a commitment to excellence, and an unwavering belief in the transformative power of positive routines. His story encourages us to embrace discipline, cultivate positive habits, and unlock the potential that lies within each of us, just as he did on the path to becoming Mr. Universe.

Chapter 7

The Magic of Mindfulness

Incorporating Mindfulness Practices for Daily Wonders

In the bustling rhythm of our daily lives, the pursuit of wonders often takes a backseat to the demands of a fast-paced world. Yet, within the folds of each passing moment lies a reservoir of magic, waiting to be discovered—a magic that unfolds when we embrace the transformative power of mindfulness in our daily practices.

Incorporating mindfulness into our routines is not merely a trend; it's an invitation to infuse every moment with a sense of purpose, connection, and profound awareness. It is a conscious choice to step away from the autopilot of habitual living and instead engage with the richness of each experience.

Begin by infusing mindfulness into your morning routine. As you wake, take a moment to appreciate the sensation of each breath, grounding yourself in the present. Allow the simple act of stretching or sipping your morning beverage to become a ritual of mindfulness, a practice that sets the tone for a day filled with wonders.

Mindful eating is another gateway to daily marvels. Instead of rushing through meals, savor each bite, relishing the textures and flavors. Notice the colors on your plate, the aromas that waft through the air, and the nourishment each morsel provides. In these moments of mindful nourishment, you cultivate a deeper connection with the sustenance that fuels your body.

In the midst of daily tasks, embrace mindfulness as a companion. Whether commuting, walking, or engaging in routine chores, allow your senses to come alive. Feel the ground beneath your feet, notice the play of light and shadow, and listen to the symphony of sounds that surround you. In these ordinary moments, extraordinary wonders unfold when approached with mindful attention.

Mindfulness practices need not be confined to dedicated sessions; they can seamlessly weave into the fabric of your day. During work or study, take mindful pauses to reset. Close your eyes, take a few conscious breaths, and bring your awareness back to the present. This simple practice enhances focus, reduces stress, and opens the door to creative insights.

Evening rituals provide yet another opportunity for mindfulness. Whether through reflective journaling, a calming meditation, or a gratitude practice, these moments of introspection create a bridge to the wonders that unfolded throughout the day. Acknowledge the small victories, moments of connection, and beauty that emerged amidst the routine.

Incorporating mindfulness practices for daily wonders is not about adding complexity to your life; it's about simplifying and deepening your engagement with each moment. As you infuse mindfulness into your daily life, you unlock a reservoir of joy, gratitude, and a heightened awareness of the wonders that exist in the ordinary. It is a journey of rediscovery—one where each day becomes a canvas for the art of living and each moment an opportunity for profound and transformative wonders.

Cultivating Present-Moment Awareness

In the perpetual dance of life, the present moment often slips through our fingers, overshadowed by the echoes of the past and the anticipation of the future. Yet, within the embrace of present-moment awareness lies a profound shift—a shift from a life lived on autopilot to one infused with depth, richness, and a profound sense of aliveness.

Cultivating present-moment awareness is not a mere practice; it is an art—an art of awakening to the vibrant symphony of the now. It begins with a conscious decision to unplug from the constant chatter of the mind and immerse oneself fully in the current moment. In doing so, we reclaim our power to shape our experiences and extract the extraordinary from the seemingly ordinary.

The journey to present-moment awareness unfolds in the simple act of conscious breathing. In each inhale and exhale, we anchor ourselves in the here and now. The breath becomes a steady rhythm, a reminder that the present moment is not an abstract concept but a tangible reality waiting to be embraced.

As we move through the day, cultivating awareness involves engaging our senses fully. Notice the play of sunlight filtering through leaves, the myriad sounds that compose the symphony of your surroundings, and the sensation of your feet meeting the ground with each step. In these sensory engagements, the richness of the present moment comes alive.

Present-moment awareness is also about releasing the grip of past regrets and future anxieties. The past, though a valuable teacher, is not a place of residence, and the future, though filled with potential, is shaped by the choices we make in the now. By letting go of the burdens of yesterday and the uncertainties of tomorrow, we free ourselves to fully inhabit the present.

In the realm of relationships, cultivating awareness transforms interactions into meaningful connections. It involves being fully present with those around us—listening actively, offering undivided attention, and savoring the shared moments. In this space of genuine connection, the beauty of human relationships unfolds.

The practice of cultivating present-moment awareness is a journey, not a destination. It requires patience, self-compassion, and a commitment to returning to the present whenever the mind wanders. The more we engage with this practice, the more it becomes an integral part of our being—a lens through which we perceive and experience life.

In conclusion, cultivating present-moment awareness is an invitation to step out of the shadows of the past and the haze of the future. It is a conscious choice to inhabit the present fully—to feel the pulse of life, savor its nuances, and dance with its ever-changing rhythm. As we embrace this art of awareness, we unlock the gateway to a life that is not merely lived but deeply experienced—a life where the richness of each moment becomes a source of joy, gratitude, and profound fulfillment.

How Mindfulness Enhances Clarity and Creativity

In the relentless pace of the modern world, where distractions abound and demands tug at our attention, the pursuit of clarity and creativity can often feel like an elusive quest. Yet, within the practice of mindfulness lies a powerful key—an instrument that not only unlocks the door to heightened awareness but also serves as a catalyst for enhancing clarity and unleashing the boundless reservoirs of creativity within.

At its essence, mindfulness is the art of being fully present—engaging with the current moment without judgment or attachment. As we cultivate this state of mindful awareness, the fog of mental clutter begins to lift, revealing a landscape of clarity that allows us to perceive situations with a fresh perspective.

Mindfulness heightens clarity by creating a space for focused attention. In a world saturated with stimuli, the ability to direct our attention to the present moment becomes a precious skill. Through mindfulness practices such as breath awareness and meditation, we learn to anchor our attention in the here and now, cutting through the noise of distractions and honing our ability to focus with clarity.

The practice of mindfulness also unravels the knots of stress and mental chatter that cloud our thinking. As we become attuned to the rhythm of our breath and the sensations in our body, the grip of anxiety loosens, and the mind finds a serene stillness. In this calm abode, clarity emerges as a natural byproduct—a clarity that allows us to approach challenges with a composed and centered mind.

Furthermore, mindfulness is a gateway to tapping into the wellspring of creativity that resides within each of us. Creativity is not a distant muse; it is an inherent aspect of human nature waiting to be ignited. By fostering a mindful mindset, we cultivate the conditions for creativity to flourish.

Mindfulness enhances creativity by fostering a non-judgmental awareness of our thoughts and ideas. In this space of acceptance, creativity is liberated from the shackles of self-doubt and criticism. We become open to exploring new perspectives, experimenting with novel concepts, and embracing the uncertainty that often accompanies the creative process.

The connection between mindfulness and creativity extends to the present moment itself. As we engage fully with each moment, we unlock a treasure trove of inspiration. The sights, sounds, and textures of the present become raw materials for creative expression. Mindfulness transforms routine moments into canvases for artistic exploration.

In conclusion, the integration of mindfulness into our lives becomes a transformative journey—a journey toward enhanced clarity and unleashed creativity. As we embrace the art of being present, we discover that clarity is not a distant destination but a lens through which we can perceive the world with greater acuity. Simultaneously, creativity is not a rare phenomenon but an inherent capacity waiting to be nurtured and released. Through mindfulness, we embark on a path of profound self-discovery—one that leads to the clarity needed to navigate life's complexities and the creativity to infuse our journey with innovation, imagination, and the boundless wonders that arise when we cultivate a mindful and creative spirit.

Anecdote Episode - 7

In the bustling academic corridors of the University of Massachusetts Medical School in the late 1970s, a quiet revolution was taking shape, led by a young molecular biologist named Jon Kabat-Zinn. Little did he know that his exploration into the realms of mindfulness meditation would pave the way for a transformative movement that would touch the lives of millions.

Jon Kabat-Zinn's journey into the world of mindfulness was shaped by a confluence of factors, beginning with his deep immersion in the rigorous world of academia. Born on June 5, 1944, in New York City, Kabat-Zinn demonstrated an early aptitude for science. He pursued his education at the Massachusetts Institute of Technology (MIT), where he earned a doctorate in molecular biology in the early 1970s.

As a young scientist, Kabat-Zinn found himself deeply entrenched in the demands of academia and the pursuit of scientific understanding. However, amidst the academic rigor, he had a profound realization—a realization that would alter the course of his life and contribute to a paradigm shift in how individuals approached health and well-being.

Observing the toll that chronic stress took on individuals within the academic and medical environments, Kabat-Zinn became acutely aware of the interconnectedness between mental and physical health. This awareness led him to recognize a critical gap in the prevailing healthcare system, which often focused on treating specific ailments without addressing the broader spectrum of factors influencing well-being.

Motivated by this insight, Kabat-Zinn embarked on a personal and professional odyssey that sought to bridge the gap between conventional medicine and holistic well-being practices. He delved into the ancient teachings of mindfulness, drawing inspiration from Eastern contemplative traditions, particularly Buddhism. Kabat-Zinn saw mindfulness not as a religious practice but as a universal and accessible tool for promoting mental clarity, emotional balance, and overall health.

In 1979, Kabat-Zinn founded the Mindfulness-Based Stress Reduction (MBSR) program at the University of Massachusetts Medical School. This program represented a pioneering effort to integrate mindfulness practices into mainstream medicine, offering a structured and evidence-based approach to stress reduction. The MBSR program included mindfulness meditation, gentle yoga, and awareness training, emphasizing the cultivation of present-moment awareness as a means to cope with stress.

Kabat-Zinn's decision to introduce mindfulness into the medical realm was initially met with skepticism. However, his dedication and belief in the transformative power of mindfulness persisted. The success of the MBSR program, coupled with the growing body of scientific evidence supporting mindfulness, gradually earned him recognition and acclaim within the medical and scientific communities.

The backdrop of Kabat-Zinn's journey was a changing cultural landscape in the 1970s, marked by an increasing interest in holistic health practices and a broader societal shift toward self-awareness and personal growth. In this context, Kabat-Zinn's work became a catalyst for a mindful revolution, demonstrating that mindfulness was not only a practice for spiritual seekers but a practical and effective approach to enhancing overall well-being.

MBSR was not merely a collection of meditation techniques; it was a comprehensive program that combined mindfulness meditation, yoga, and awareness training. Kabat-Zinn's approach was rooted in the idea that cultivating present-moment awareness could empower individuals to respond more skillfully to the challenges of life, alleviating stress and promoting a deeper sense of well-being.

The impact of Kabat-Zinn's work quickly became apparent. Participants in the MBSR program reported reduced stress levels, improved focus, and a greater sense of emotional balance. The mindful revolution that began in the hallowed halls of academia soon expanded beyond academia, reaching diverse communities and individuals grappling with the demands of modern life.

As the efficacy of MBSR gained recognition, Kabat-Zinn's influence extended beyond the academic sphere. He published the landmark book "Full Catastrophe Living," which introduced mindfulness principles to a broader audience. The program, once met with skepticism, became a cornerstone of integrative medicine, embraced by healthcare professionals, psychologists, and individuals seeking a holistic approach to health.

Kabat-Zinn's journey illustrates not only the power of mindfulness to alleviate stress but also its capacity to enhance overall well-being. His work became a catalyst for a broader cultural shift, encouraging individuals to embrace mindfulness not as a mere technique but as a way of life. Through the MBSR program, countless lives were touched, and the transformative impact of mindfulness on mental, emotional, and physical health became irrefutable.

Today, Jon Kabat-Zinn's legacy persists. MBSR has become a globally recognized program, and mindfulness has woven its way into diverse fields, from psychology to education and beyond. Kabat-Zinn's quiet revolution has left an indelible mark, reminding individuals that the practice of mindfulness is not just a remedy for stress but a gateway to a more conscious, resilient, and fulfilled existence. Through his pioneering efforts, he has invited the world to join the mindful revolution and experience the wonders that unfold when we bring our full attention to the present moment.

Chapter 8

The Wonders of Connection

Building Meaningful Relationships for Mutual Growth

In life, one of the most fulfilling endeavors is the art of building meaningful relationships. Far beyond mere connections, these bonds become conduits for mutual growth, shared aspirations, and the cultivation of a rich canvas of shared experiences. Building meaningful relationships is not just a social skill; it is a profound journey of self-discovery, empathy, and the creation of a collective narrative that transcends individual stories.

At the heart of meaningful relationships lies authenticity—an unwavering commitment to showing up as your true self and embracing others in their authenticity. When we bring our genuine selves into relationships, vulnerabilities and all, we create a foundation of trust that forms the bedrock for mutual growth. Authenticity fosters a deep sense of connection, allowing both individuals to flourish in an environment of acceptance and understanding.

Listening becomes the cornerstone of building meaningful relationships. Beyond hearing words, true listening involves tuning into the emotions, nuances, and unspoken sentiments that weave through conversations. It is the art of being fully present with others, creating a space where they feel heard, valued, and seen. In this shared space of genuine listening, relationships blossom into vessels for mutual understanding and growth.

Reciprocity is a key ingredient in meaningful relationships. It is the understanding that growth is not a solitary journey; it is a shared expedition where each individual contributes to the other's development. In the give-and-take of support, encouragement, and shared experiences, relationships become dynamic platforms for mutual elevation.

Meaningful relationships thrive on shared values and common goals. When individuals align their aspirations, dreams, and values, a synergy emerges that propels both parties toward collective growth. This shared purpose becomes a driving force, infusing the relationship with a sense of meaning and direction.

Empathy, the ability to step into another's shoes and understand their perspective, becomes a bridge to meaningful connections. It is the recognition that each person carries their own unique journey, challenges, and triumphs. Through empathy, relationships become vessels for compassion, kindness, and the powerful recognition of each other's humanity.

Building meaningful relationships requires an investment of time and energy. It involves being present in both the triumphs and tribulations of those we connect with. Celebrating achievements and offering support during challenges solidifies the bonds and creates a network of resilience that withstands the tests of time.

Ultimately, meaningful relationships are a testament to the richness of the human experience. They transcend the superficial layers of social interactions, delving into the depths of shared emotions, aspirations, and growth. As we embark on the journey of building meaningful relationships, we discover that by fostering the growth of others, we cultivate our own. It is a dance of mutual inspiration, an exchange that transforms both individuals, and a reminder that the beauty of life is magnified when shared with those who contribute to our journey of becoming our best selves.

The Impact of Social Support on Personal Development

In the intricate mosaic of personal development, one of the most influential forces is the impact of social support—a dynamic interplay that shapes, nurtures, and propels individuals toward their highest potential. Far beyond a mere network of connections, social support becomes a cornerstone for resilience, growth, and the cultivation of a life infused with purpose and fulfillment.

At its essence, social support is a tapestry of relationships—family, friends, mentors, and communities—that forms a safety net beneath the tightrope of life. It is the understanding that, in the vast expanse of human experience, individuals are not solitary islands but interconnected beings whose journeys are enriched by the meaningful relationships that surround them.

The impact of social support on personal development is profound, beginning with the buoyancy it provides during challenging times. Life is replete with trials and tribulations, and in these moments of adversity, social support becomes a source of strength. Whether through the comforting presence of loved ones, the wisdom of mentors, or the camaraderie of a supportive community, individuals find solace and courage to navigate the stormy seas of life.

Beyond emotional sustenance, social support offers a mirror—a reflection of one's potential, capabilities, and unique qualities. Encouragement from those who believe in our abilities becomes a catalyst for self-belief. In the echo of supportive voices, individuals discover the courage to pursue their aspirations, overcome self-doubt, and step into the fullness of their potential.

Social support acts as a catalyst for personal growth through shared learning and collective wisdom. In the exchange of experiences, insights, and perspectives, individuals benefit from the collective knowledge of their social network. Mentors provide guidance, friends offer diverse viewpoints, and communities become classrooms for life's invaluable lessons.

Moreover, social support nurtures a sense of belonging—an intrinsic human need that fuels personal development. The knowledge that one is part of a community, a family, or a network of friends creates a foundation of security. In this sense of belonging, individuals feel empowered to explore, take risks, and embark on the transformative journey of self-discovery.

Celebrations become more joyful and burdens lighter when shared within the tapestry of social support. Achievements are magnified by the applause of those who genuinely celebrate success, and challenges are softened by the collective strength of a supportive network. In this interconnected dance, personal development is not a solitary endeavor but a shared symphony where the harmonies of growth resonate throughout the collective.

In conclusion, the impact of social support on personal development is a testament to the interconnected nature of the human experience. As individuals traverse the landscape of growth, the relationships that form their social support system become pillars of strength, sources of inspiration, and mirrors reflecting the boundless potential that resides within. In the embrace of social support, personal development becomes a collaborative masterpiece—a shared journey where the echoes of encouragement, the lessons of collective wisdom, and the warmth of human connection create a canvas painted with the vibrant hues of resilience, growth, and the extraordinary impact of a supportive community.

Networking Strategies for Opening Doors to New Opportunities

In personal and professional growth, few skills hold the transformative power of effective networking. Beyond a mere exchange of business cards or digital connections, strategic networking becomes a dynamic force—a conduit for opening doors to new opportunities, forging meaningful relationships, and navigating the labyrinth of success.

At its core, networking is not a transaction but a relational art—a genuine effort to connect, collaborate, and create a network of relationships that transcends superficial interactions. In the realm of personal development, effective networking is a skill that propels individuals toward the opportunities they seek, creating a ripple effect that extends far beyond the initial point of connection.

Strategic networking begins with authenticity—a commitment to being genuine and building connections rooted in mutual respect. It involves showcasing one's unique strengths, experiences, and aspirations without pretense. Authenticity forms the bedrock of lasting connections, as individuals resonate with the sincerity of those they meet.

Listening becomes a superpower in the art of networking. Beyond the exchange of information, active listening involves tuning into the needs, challenges, and goals of others. By understanding the perspectives of those within one's network, individuals can identify opportunities for collaboration, support, and shared growth.

Strategic networking thrives on the principle of reciprocity. It's not just about what one can gain but also about what one can contribute to the network. By offering support, insights, and assistance to others, individuals contribute to the collective strength of their network, fostering a culture of collaboration and shared success.

In the digital age, online platforms serve as powerful arenas for strategic networking. However, the essence of meaningful connections remains rooted in personal interactions. Face-to-face meetings, whether in professional events, community gatherings, or informal settings, provide opportunities to forge deeper connections, convey authenticity, and leave a lasting impression.

Effective networking involves nurturing relationships over time. It's not about collecting an extensive list of contacts but cultivating a network of genuine connections. Consistent follow-ups, expressing genuine interest in others' journeys, and providing support when possible contribute to the longevity and depth of networking relationships.

Networking is also about leveraging diverse perspectives. A robust network includes individuals from various industries, backgrounds, and experiences. This diversity not only enriches one's own perspective but also opens doors to a myriad of opportunities that may not have been visible within a more homogeneous network.

Opportunities often arise in unexpected places. A chance conversation, a shared interest, or a collaborative project can be the catalyst for transformative opportunities. By maintaining an open mind and being receptive to the possibilities that emerge within one's network, individuals position themselves to seize unforeseen prospects.

In conclusion, networking is a dynamic force that propels individuals beyond the confines of their individual capabilities. As a strategic skill in personal development, effective networking is not about quantity but quality, not about transactions but relationships. It's a journey of authenticity, reciprocity, and cultivating a network that becomes a gateway to new horizons. In the tapestry of personal and professional growth, the art of strategic networking becomes a brushstroke that paints a canvas of endless possibilities—a canvas where doors to new opportunities swing wide open, and the journey of success becomes a collaborative dance within a network of genuine and impactful connections.

Anecdote Episode - 8

In the quiet town of Tuscumbia, Alabama, on June 27, 1880, a child was born into a world of silence and darkness. Little did anyone know that this child, named Helen Keller, would defy the odds, break barriers, and become an enduring symbol of resilience and triumph over adversity.

Helen Keller's early years were marked by profound challenges. At the tender age of 19 months, an illness left her deaf and blind, closing the doors to the world of communication and understanding. Trapped in a realm of isolation, young Helen faced a seemingly insurmountable obstacle—until the arrival of a determined and patient teacher, Anne Sullivan.

Anne Sullivan, herself visually impaired, arrived in the Keller household in March 1887. What ensued was a remarkable journey of connection, understanding, and unbreakable bonds. Anne began the arduous task of teaching Helen to communicate by spelling words into her hand using the manual alphabet. It was through this tactile method that the first rays of comprehension dawned on Helen, unlocking the world of language and knowledge.

The early days were challenging, marked by frustration and resistance. Helen, accustomed to a world of silence and darkness, struggled to comprehend the significance of the signs her teacher was imparting. However, Anne Sullivan's unwavering dedication and belief in Helen's potential became the cornerstone of their relationship.

The breakthrough came at the water pump in the Keller family's backyard. As Anne spelled "water" into Helen's hand while water flowed over her other hand, Helen made the connection between the word and the tangible reality before her. In that moment, the barriers began to crumble, and Helen Keller's journey of discovery commenced.

Anne Sullivan's role extended beyond teaching; she became Helen's mentor, friend, and constant companion. Together, they embarked on a rigorous educational journey, defying societal expectations for individuals with disabilities. Helen learned to read Braille, write, and speak. She excelled academically, graduating with honors from Radcliffe College in 1904, becoming the first deaf-blind person to earn a Bachelor of Arts degree.

The lifelong connection between Helen Keller and Anne Sullivan was a testament to the transformative power of meaningful relationships. Anne not only taught Helen language but also instilled in her a sense of purpose, resilience, and the belief that obstacles could be overcome. Their bond went beyond the teacher-student relationship; it was a profound friendship built on trust, understanding, and shared triumphs.

Helen Keller's impact extended beyond her personal achievements. She became a tireless advocate for people with disabilities, a champion of social justice, and a global ambassador for the blind and deaf. Through her lectures, writings, and activism, Keller inspired countless individuals to see beyond physical limitations and recognize the untapped potential within themselves.

In June 1968, Helen Keller passed away, leaving behind a legacy that continues to resonate. Her life exemplifies the transformative power of social support and meaningful connections in overcoming adversity. Helen Keller's unbreakable bonds with Anne Sullivan remain an enduring testament to the possibilities that unfold when individuals, no matter the challenges they face, are supported by unwavering companionship and belief in their inherent potential.

Chapter 9

The Wonder of Balance

Nurturing a Well-Balanced Life

In the whirlwind of modern life, the pursuit of a well-balanced existence is not just a goal—it is an art, a delicate dance that requires conscious choices, intentional living, and a commitment to prioritizing well-being amidst the myriad demands. Nurturing a well-balanced life is not about juggling competing priorities but about orchestrating a symphony where each element harmonizes to create a life of fulfillment, purpose, and sustained vitality.

At the core of a well-balanced life lies the art of self-care. It is the recognition that caring for oneself is not a luxury but a necessity—a foundational pillar upon which all other aspects of life are built. Whether through moments of solitude, rejuvenating activities, or practices that nourish the body and mind, taking care of yourself is the cornerstone of resilience and vitality.

Balance emanates from the conscious allocation of time and energy to various facets of life. It involves setting boundaries, learning to say no when necessary, and recognizing that a well-balanced life is not about doing it all but about doing what matters most. Prioritization becomes a compass that guides individuals toward activities aligned with their values and overarching life goals.

A well-balanced life also thrives on the cultivation of meaningful relationships. In the tapestry of existence, connections with loved ones, friends, and the community provide a support system that enhances emotional well-being. Nurturing relationships involves both giving and receiving, creating a dynamic exchange that contributes to a sense of belonging and shared joy.

The pursuit of balance extends to professional endeavors. It is about finding the equilibrium between work and personal life, recognizing that overcommitment and burnout are adversaries to well-being. Setting realistic goals, establishing boundaries, and embracing moments of rest are integral to a sustainable and fulfilling career journey.

Physical health is an indispensable component of a well-balanced life. Regular exercise, a balanced diet, and sufficient sleep contribute to overall well-being, providing the energy and vitality needed to engage fully in life's pursuits. A well-nourished body becomes the canvas upon which a well-balanced life is painted.

Mindfulness practices play a vital role in nurturing balance. The ability to be present in each moment, to savor the richness of experiences without being entangled in past regrets or future anxieties, becomes a gateway to a well-balanced life. Mindfulness instills a sense of calm and clarity, fostering resilience in the face of life's inevitable challenges.

A well-balanced life is not a static destination but a continual process of recalibration. It involves periodic self-reflection, assessment of priorities, and adaptation to the evolving landscape of one's life. Flexibility becomes a key attribute, allowing individuals to navigate changes with grace and resilience.

In conclusion, nurturing a well-balanced life is an ongoing journey—a journey that unfolds in the daily choices, the relationships fostered, and the intentional alignment of activities with personal values. It is an art that requires self-awareness, prioritization, and a commitment to well-being. In the symphony of life, a well-balanced existence becomes a melody—a harmonious composition where self-care, meaningful connections, and a mindful approach converge to create a life that is not just lived but lived well, with purpose, fulfillment, and an enduring sense of vitality.

Balancing Professional and Personal Aspects

In life, one of the most challenging yet rewarding feats is the delicate art of balancing professional and personal aspects. As the demands of the professional realm intertwine with the joys and responsibilities of personal life, the pursuit of equilibrium becomes a journey of self-discovery, intentional choices, and the cultivation of a life that resonates with fulfillment on both fronts.

At the heart of this pursuit lies the art of setting boundaries. It is the conscious recognition that professional success and personal well-being are not mutually exclusive but interconnected facets of a holistic life. Setting boundaries involves delineating dedicated spaces and times for work and personal activities, ensuring that one does not overshadow the other.

Communication becomes a linchpin in the delicate balance between the professional and personal realms. Open and honest communication with colleagues, supervisors, and family members fosters understanding and support. Sharing expectations, setting realistic priorities, and expressing needs contribute to a harmonious integration of both aspects of life.

Prioritization emerges as a guiding principle in the quest for balance. It involves discerning between what is urgent and what is important, recognizing that not all tasks carry equal weight. By identifying and prioritizing tasks based on their significance, individuals can allocate time and energy efficiently, achieving a sense of accomplishment in both professional and personal pursuits.

Flexibility becomes an invaluable ally in the pursuit of balance. Life is dynamic, and unexpected challenges or opportunities may arise. Embracing flexibility means being adaptable in the face of change, adjusting plans when necessary, and navigating the ebb and flow of both professional and personal landscapes with resilience and grace.

Work-life integration, rather than strict compartmentalization, offers a holistic approach to balancing professional and personal aspects. It involves finding synergies between work and personal activities, incorporating elements of well-being into the professional routine, and recognizing that both aspects contribute to a multifaceted, fulfilling life.

Self-care becomes non-negotiable in the quest for balance. It is the understanding that personal well-being is the foundation upon which professional success is built. Regular breaks, moments of rejuvenation, and self-reflection become essential practices that nourish the mind, body, and spirit, fostering resilience in the face of life's demands.

In the pursuit of balance, the power of saying 'no' becomes a liberating force. It involves recognizing personal limits, understanding one's capacity, and being selective about commitments. Saying 'no' is not a sign of weakness but a declaration of self-awareness and a commitment to maintaining equilibrium in the face of competing demands.

Celebrating achievements, both big and small, becomes a cornerstone of a balanced life. Whether it's a professional milestone or a personal accomplishment, acknowledging and savoring successes contributes to a positive mindset and reinforces a sense of balance in the overall journey.

In conclusion, balancing professional and personal aspects is not a static destination but an ongoing journey—an intricate dance that evolves with each step taken. It requires self-awareness, effective communication, and a commitment to well-being. In the harmonious blend of work and personal life, individuals find not just balance but a life that resonates with purpose, fulfillment, and the extraordinary richness that comes from navigating the dynamic interplay of professional and personal realms with intention, resilience, and a genuine zest for life.

The Synergy of Balance in Achieving Remarkable Feats

In human achievements, there exists a profound truth—a truth that transcends the hustle and bustle of relentless pursuit and speaks to the essence of lasting success. It is the understanding that behind every remarkable feat lies the synergy of balance—a delicate interplay between focused determination, well-being, and the harmonious integration of various life facets.

The concept of balance in achieving remarkable feats is not about compromise or settling for mediocrity; rather, it is a dynamic equilibrium that propels individuals to new heights of excellence. It is the recognition that sustainable success goes hand in hand with a well-nurtured mind, body, and spirit.

At the heart of this synergy is the art of prioritization. It involves discerning between tasks that contribute to the overarching goal and those that merely clamor for attention. By focusing energy on what truly matters, individuals channel their efforts into a streamlined path of achievement, ensuring that each step aligns with their vision of success.

Balance, in the context of remarkable feats, is a proactive choice to cultivate resilience. It is the acknowledgment that life's journey is dotted with challenges, setbacks, and unforeseen twists. By maintaining equilibrium, individuals not only weather the storms with grace but also emerge stronger, armed with the lessons and insights gained through the ebb and flow of their endeavors.

In the pursuit of remarkable feats, the synergy of balance extends beyond the professional realm. It encompasses the nourishment of personal relationships, physical health, and emotional well-being. A holistic approach to achievement recognizes that success is not compartmentalized but a reflection of one's entire life—each facet contributing to the brilliance of the whole.

Mindfulness becomes a guiding light in this intricate dance of balance. It involves being fully present in the journey, appreciating the milestones achieved, and savoring the nuances of the process. By fostering a mindful approach, individuals infuse their actions with intention, clarity, and a profound connection to the present moment.

The synergy of balance is also about acknowledging the power of rest and rejuvenation. In the relentless pursuit of goals, the replenishment of energy is not a luxury but a strategic necessity. Moments of pause, whether in the form of breaks, hobbies, or quiet reflection, become integral to sustaining the vigor needed for remarkable feats.

In the collaborative symphony of achievements, effective communication plays a pivotal role. It involves expressing needs, setting boundaries, and seeking support from those in one's personal and professional circles. Open dialogue fosters an environment where individuals feel empowered to pursue their aspirations without sacrificing their overall well-being.

Celebrating milestones along the journey becomes a source of motivation and inspiration. Recognizing achievements, no matter how small, reinforces the sense of progress and fuels the momentum needed for the pursuit of remarkable feats. It is a reminder that each step, each effort, contributes to the grand picture of success.

In conclusion, the synergy of balance is not an elusive ideal but a tangible force that underlies every remarkable feat. It is a dynamic dance—a conscious integration of focused effort, holistic well-being, and a mindful approach to the journey. In the pursuit of extraordinary accomplishments, individuals discover that true success is not a destination but a transformative journey—a journey where the synergy of balance becomes the guiding principle, propelling them to feats that not only stand as testaments to their capabilities but also resonate with lasting fulfillment and a life well-lived.

Anecdote Episode - 9

In the heart of the coal-mining town of Raniganj, where the earth bore witness to the toil of miners and the shadows of the mines painted the landscape, there unfolded a tale of resilience and the remarkable human spirit. It was a day like any other, with the rhythmic sounds of pickaxes echoing in the tunnels, when disaster struck. A section of the mine collapsed, trapping a group of miners deep within its unforgiving embrace. Panic swept through the community, and as the dust settled, it seemed hope had been buried alongside the miners.

Amidst the chaos, a figure emerged: a man named Vikram Singh, known for his unwavering determination and an uncanny ability to navigate the labyrinthine tunnels of the mines. Vikram, a seasoned miner himself, took charge of what seemed like an insurmountable rescue mission. The atmosphere was heavy with despair, but Vikram's eyes reflected a steely resolve that cut through the darkness.

The authorities, initially hesitant, entrusted Vikram with the task of leading the mission. Armed with nothing but a battered map of the mine and a flickering lantern, he delved into the depths where others feared to tread. The rescue mission wasn't just about physically extracting trapped bodies; it became a quest to revive the flickering flame of hope in the hearts of the community.

As Vikram navigated the narrow passages, he encountered challenges that would daunt even the bravest souls. The mine, like a subterranean maze, seemed to conspire against their efforts. But Vikram, fueled by a deep-rooted belief that miracles could happen even in the darkest depths, pressed on.

Days turned into nights, and hope flickered like a fragile flame. Yet, Vikram's leadership brought a spark of resilience to the rescue team. He orchestrated a synchronized dance of efforts, turning chaos into coordinated determination. Each miner rescued was a victory snatched from the jaws of despair, and each step forward resonated with the heartbeat of the entire community.

Through tunnels that seemed to weave tales of hardship, Vikram led the rescue mission with a blend of expertise and an almost spiritual connection to the underground world. It was as if he could decipher the language of the earth and guide his team to where hope still clung to the walls.

Finally, after what felt like an eternity, the last miner emerged from the darkness, blinking against the sudden flood of light. The town of Raniganj erupted in joy, and tears of relief flowed freely. Vikram, now a beacon of inspiration, stood amidst the crowd, his worn hands a testament to the sweat and determination that had brought about this miracle.

The Raniganj mission wasn't just a rescue; it was a testament to the wonders that can be achieved when one person decides to defy the odds. Vikram Singh, the hero of Raniganj, had regulated a mission that transcended the physical act of saving lives; he had reignited hope, proving that even in the depths of despair, wonders can be worked with a heart aflame with courage.

Chapter 10

Wonders in Action

Applying the Principles of Wonders to Real-Life Situations

In life, the principles of wonder are not distant concepts reserved for fairy tales; they are guiding forces that, when applied to real-life situations, have the power to transform the ordinary into the extraordinary. It is the recognition that the magic of wonders lies not in wishful thinking but in the intentional application of principles that amplify the richness of human experience.

One fundamental principle is the art of gratitude. In real-life situations, gratitude is not just a fleeting emotion but a transformative practice that enhances perspective and cultivates a positive mindset. By consciously acknowledging and appreciating the blessings, both big and small, individuals infuse their daily lives with a sense of abundance and joy.

The principle of resilience takes center stage when faced with challenges. Real-life situations are riddled with obstacles, setbacks, and moments of adversity. Applying the principle of resilience involves not merely bouncing back but bouncing forward—learning, growing, and evolving through the challenges. It is the understanding that within every setback lies an opportunity for greater strength and wisdom.

Mindfulness becomes a guiding light in navigating the complexities of real-life situations. It is the practice of being fully present, free from the entanglements of past regrets or future anxieties. By applying mindfulness, individuals engage with the current moment with heightened awareness, allowing for better decision-making, reduced stress, and a deeper appreciation for the nuances of life.

The principle of adaptation is crucial in the face of change. Real-life situations are dynamic, and the ability to adapt is not a sign of weakness but a demonstration of resilience and resourcefulness. Embracing change with an open mind and a flexible attitude allows individuals to navigate uncertainties with grace and creativity.

Kindness, often underestimated in its power, emerges as a transformative force in real-life interactions. Applying the principle of kindness involves not only being kind to others but also extending kindness to oneself. In the ebb and flow of daily life, acts of kindness create a butterfly effect, fostering connection, understanding, and a positive atmosphere.

Real-life situations provide ample opportunities to apply the principle of intentionality. It is a conscious decision to align actions with values and goals. By approaching tasks, relationships, and endeavors with intention, individuals infuse purpose into their actions, ensuring that each step contributes meaningfully to their overarching objectives.

The principle of growth is a continuous thread woven into the fabric of real-life experiences. It involves embracing a mindset of continuous learning, self-discovery, and evolution. Realizing that every experience, whether positive or challenging, contributes to personal and professional growth fosters a sense of purpose and fulfillment.

Connection, both with oneself and others, is a cornerstone in applying the principles of wonder to real-life situations. Cultivating genuine connections involves active listening, empathy, and the willingness to understand diverse perspectives. By fostering meaningful connections, individuals create a supportive network that enriches their journey through life.

In conclusion, the principles of wonder are not abstract ideals but actionable tools that individuals can wield to enhance the vibrancy of real-life situations. Gratitude, resilience, mindfulness, adaptation, kindness, intentionality, and growth are not mere concepts; they are the guiding stars that illuminate the path to a life filled with purpose, fulfillment, and the extraordinary wonders that emerge when principles are consciously applied to the canvas of everyday existence.

Showcasing Inspiring Success Stories

In the vast expanse of human endeavor, success stories stand as beacons of inspiration—testaments to the resilience, determination, and unwavering spirit that resides within each individual. Showcasing these inspiring narratives is not merely a recounting of achievements; it is a powerful tool that ignites the spark of possibility, offering a roadmap for others to embark on their own journeys of triumph.

At the heart of inspiring success stories lies the universal truth that success is not exclusive to a select few but is within reach for anyone willing to embrace the journey. These stories illuminate the diverse paths individuals traverse, dispelling the notion that there is a singular formula for success. Instead, they showcase the myriad ways people have overcome challenges, seized opportunities, and carved their unique paths to achievement.

One crucial aspect of success stories is the acknowledgment of setbacks and challenges. The road to triumph is rarely smooth, and inspiring narratives often reveal moments of adversity, doubt, and perseverance. By shedding light on the hurdles individuals face, these stories become a source of reassurance and empowerment for those navigating their own challenges.

Inspiring success stories underscore the power of resilience. They demonstrate that setbacks are not roadblocks but stepping stones, opportunities for growth, and invitations to tap into untapped reservoirs of strength. Each story paints a vivid picture of individuals who, in the face of adversity, chose to rise, adapt, and continue their journey toward success.

The diversity of success stories also showcases the multiplicity of definitions of success. Beyond traditional notions of wealth or fame, these narratives encompass personal fulfillment, social impact, and contributions to the greater good. Inspiring success stories redefine success as a holistic concept—one that aligns with individual values, passions, and aspirations.

Moreover, these stories highlight the role of continuous learning and evolution. Success is not a static destination but a dynamic journey of growth and self-discovery.

Individuals in these narratives exemplify the spirit of lifelong learners, constantly evolving, adapting, and refining their skills to stay relevant and impactful in their chosen fields.

Inspiring success stories bridge the gap between aspiration and realization. They serve as tangible evidence that dreams are achievable, that goals are within grasp, and that the pursuit of one's passion can lead to a fulfilling and successful life. By showcasing relatable role models, these stories empower individuals to believe in their potential and take courageous steps toward their own aspirations.

In conclusion, the impact is profound. It is a narrative that transcends individual achievements, reaching into the hearts and minds of those who seek inspiration. These stories become a collective testament to the human spirit—a reminder that success is not an exclusive club but an inclusive journey open to all. As individuals absorb these narratives, they are not merely witnesses; they become participants in the grand theater of success, each act adding a unique story that adds to the collective inspiration and motivation for others to embark on their own extraordinary journeys of triumph.

Your Blueprint for Unleashing Continuous Wonders

In life, there exists a blueprint—an intricate guide that, when followed with intention and dedication, has the power to unleash continuous wonders. This blueprint is not a rigid set of rules but a dynamic framework that empowers individuals to navigate the complexities of their journey, unlocking the extraordinary in the ordinary and savoring the richness of each moment.

At the foundation of your blueprint for continuous wonder lies the principle of self-discovery. It is the recognition that the journey to continuous wonders begins within. Take the time to explore the depths of your passions, strengths, and values. By understanding who you are at your core, you lay the groundwork for a life that resonates with authenticity and purpose.

Embrace the power of curiosity as the cornerstone of your blueprint. Cultivate a mindset that thrives on exploration and a genuine interest in the world around you. Approach each day with an open heart and a willingness to discover the beauty hidden in the ordinary. In curiosity, you find the key to unlocking the door to continuous wonders.

The art of resilience is woven into the fabric of your blueprint. Recognize that challenges are not roadblocks but opportunities for growth. Embrace setbacks as stepping stones, and let resilience be the force that propels you forward. By facing adversity with courage and determination, you pave the way for wonders to unfold in unexpected ways.

Mindfulness becomes a guiding star in your blueprint for continuous wonders. Be fully present in each moment, appreciating the richness of experiences without being entangled in past regrets or future anxieties. In mindfulness, you discover a sanctuary of peace and clarity—a space where wonders reveal themselves in the simple act of being.

Connection, both with yourself and others, is a vital thread in your blueprint. Nurture meaningful relationships that uplift and inspire. Recognize the shared humanity that binds us all and find wonders in the tapestry of connections. By fostering a network of support and understanding, you create a foundation for continuous wonders to flourish.

Your blueprint for continuous wonders involves the intentional cultivation of gratitude. Take a moment each day to reflect on the blessings that surround you. In gratitude, you amplify the positive aspects of your life, fostering a mindset that attracts wonders and abundance. A heart filled with gratitude becomes a magnet for continuous joy.

Strive for growth as an integral part of your blueprint. Continuous wonders unfold in the expanses of self-improvement and learning. Embrace new opportunities, acquire new skills, and challenge yourself to evolve. In the journey of growth, you open doors to wonders that align with the ever-changing landscape of your aspirations.

Celebrate small victories along your path. Your blueprint for continuous wonders is dotted with milestones, both big and small. Acknowledge and savor each achievement, recognizing that every step forward is a triumph. In celebration, you fuel the momentum for more wonders to manifest in your life.

In conclusion, your blueprint for continuous wonders is a living document—a guide that evolves with your journey. It is a reflection of your values, aspirations, and the innate potential within you. As you navigate the complexities of life, keep this blueprint in your heart, allowing it to be a compass that guides you toward continuous wonders. In each choice, each moment of mindfulness, and each connection forged, you unleash the extraordinary—a life filled with wonders that cascade in a continuous, harmonious symphony.

Anecdotal Episode - 10

In the brisk December of 1996, I [Manoj Dembla] found myself at the helm of a financial storm. Freshly appointed as the financial controller for the Haryana Circle for a telecom firm entwined in a joint venture with a multinational corporation closely associated with Hong Kong, I was faced with a daunting challenge.

The global accounting of the company demanded an immediate merger, setting a deadline of December 31, 1996. Yet, here in India, our accounting systems followed a different rhythm, preferring the ideas of March for such financial reckonings. The clash of timelines presented a conundrum that needed immediate resolution.

As the clock relentlessly ticked away, I called upon the entire staff of my accounting office spread across the districts of Haryana. Gathered in our regional office in Sonipat, we faced a mountain of accounts demanding attention. The working hours left were a mere 7-8, a paltry window for the colossal task ahead.

With determination burning bright, we embarked on an extraordinary journey. From the afternoon into the night and through the early morning hours until the clock struck 2 PM, the next day, we toiled without respite. Sleep became a distant memory as we meticulously combed through the numbers, inching closer to the completion of our colossal task.

The results spoke volumes. Our head office, a spectator to the Herculean effort, was not just impressed; they were elated. Under my dynamic leadership, the seemingly impossible had been achieved. The triumph of overcoming insurmountable odds not only elevated my professional standing but also paved the way for a well-deserved promotion.

This success story did not fade into the archives; it became a guiding light for all those who worked beside me. The tale of resilience, teamwork, and unyielding determination became a cornerstone of motivation. Even now, as I reflect on those intense hours, it serves as a testament to the belief that the impossible is merely the unexplored.

As time marched on, more challenges presented themselves, each met with the same spirit that fueled that December night. The echoes of success stories resonate in my mind, pushing me to strive for greatness. I carry with me the conviction that no challenge is too great and that every obstacle is an opportunity waiting to be seized. In my career, these stories weave a narrative of triumph, serving as beacons of inspiration for all who tread the path after me.

Author's Biography

Manoj Dembla, one of the remarkable Chartered Accountants of India

Chartered accounting is by far one of the most challenging and highly reputed professions in India. The journey to becoming a chartered accountant is tedious, with a lot of ups and downs. Those who succeed in cracking the examination and have a thorough understanding of the field go on to become massive successes in the fields of finance and accountancy. Manoj Dembla is one such prominent name whose work ethos makes him India's best-known chartered accountant.

With his roots in Rajasthan's Bikaner and upbringing in Jaipur, the CA is currently based in Mumbai. Ever since Mr. Manoj Dembla began his career in the field of accounting and finance, he has ensured to maintain consistency with his successful academic track record. Being a gold medalist at the coveted Panjab University, he is also a rank holder and a member of the Institute of Chartered Accountants of India (ICAI).

Mr. Dembla's experience of more than three decades across different industries like automobiles, telecom, entertainment, infrastructure, and real estate makes him a profound Chartered Accountant in India. Having worked for years in the financial horizon, Manoj Dembla has a thorough knowledge of all facets of finance, accounting, statutory compliance, project financing, commercial and legal operations, and business management across diversified sectors.

Nevertheless, being the best in the business, his core expertise lies in working capital management, finalization, taxation, internal and statutory audits, liasoning, fund mobilization and treasury management, and leading group initiatives for organizational objectives. Currently, Manoj Dembla is working as an advisor in finance, accounts, and taxation at India's leading music and entertainment company, T-Series.

In the past, he has worked at Deloitte and Vodafone. Known for his out-of-the-box approach and optimistic methodology, he is considered the go-to financial person in the organization. At T-Series, he manages a myriad of activities like cash flow analysis, treasury management, and financial strategy. In addition, he works closely with the top management in planning, implementing, and processing different business operational activities. For his commendable work, he has been awarded the CFO100 Award in 2014, 2016, and 2020. Besides this, he is an author with a curious mind and a Web3 enthusiast who loves to explore different aspects of the field of finance and cryptocurrency.